Glendale Library, Arts & Culture Dept.

3 9 0 1 0 0 5 5 8 8 1 9 4 4

D0772762

NO LONGER PROPERTY OF
GLENDALE LIBRARY,
ARTS & CULTURE DEPT.

LC: Φ TC:Φ(6/19)

What Is Schizophrenia?

Melissa Abramovitz

San Diego, CA   **616.898 ABR**

About the Author

Melissa Abramovitz has been a freelance writer and author for thirty years and specializes in writing nonfiction magazine articles and books for all age groups. She is the author of hundreds of magazine articles, more than forty educational books for children and teenagers, numerous poems and short stories, several children's picture books, and a book for writers. Abramovitz graduated from the University of California–San Diego with a degree in psychology and is also a graduate of the Institute of Children's Literature.

© 2016 ReferencePoint Press, Inc.
Printed in the United States

For more information, contact:
ReferencePoint Press, Inc.
PO Box 27779
San Diego, CA 92198
www.ReferencePointPress.com

ALL RIGHTS RESERVED.
No part of this work covered by the copyright hereon may be reproduced or used in any form or by any means—graphic, electronic, or mechanical, including photocopying, recording, taping, web distribution, or information storage retrieval systems—without the written permission of the publisher.

LIBRARY OF CONGRESS CATALOGING-IN-PUBLICATION DATA

Abramovitz, Melissa, 1954-
 What is schizophrenia? / by Melissa Abramovitz.
    pages cm. -- (Understanding mental disorders)
 Audience: Grade 9 to 12.
 Includes bibliographical references and index.
 ISBN-13: 978-1-60152-926-8 (hardback)
 ISBN-10: 1-60152-926-0 (hardback)
 1. Schizophrenia--Juvenile literature. I. Title.
 RC514.A247 2016
 616.89'8--dc23
                                                      2015012261

CONTENTS

INTRODUCTION

Schizophrenia: A Personal and Societal Burden

People with schizophrenia—one of the most severe mental illnesses in the world—experience a variety of terrifying mental distortions that often render them unable to function or interact with others. Many schizophrenics are homeless, commit a variety of crimes, turn their families' lives into unending nightmares, and cost society billions of dollars and countless other resources each year. Schizophrenia is thus a significant personal and societal burden that impacts all cultures.

Personal and Economic Costs

In 1751 the British physician Richard Mead wrote in his book *Medical Precepts and Cautions*, "There is no disease more to be dreaded than madness. For what greater unhappiness can befall a man, than to be deprived of his reason and understanding; to attack his fellow-creatures with fury like a wild beast; to be tied down, and even beat; ... to fancy hobgoblins haunting him."[1] Even though schizophrenia was not so named until 1911, Mead's description of what was known as "madness" clearly portrays some of the symptoms and behaviors that characterize schizophrenia.

Although medical science has progressed a great deal since Mead's time, the difficulties faced by schizophrenics and the effects of the disease on society have not changed all that much. There is no cure, and schizophrenia usually lasts a lifetime once it presents (usually in adolescence or young adulthood). Today some patients who take their prescribed medications are able to lead fulfilling and productive lives, but these medications are not effective for everyone. In addition up to 70 percent of those who receive treatment do not take their medications for various reasons, such as the drugs' side effects and a lack of awareness about one's illness.

Thus, although effective drugs have been available since the 1950s, these have not diminished schizophrenia's personal and societal burdens as much as experts hoped. According to psychiatrist Mark Olfson, even with treatment, most patients experience ongoing symptoms that make schizophrenia "among the most disabling of all medical conditions. The World Health Organization, for example, ranks schizophrenia as more disabling than amputation of both legs, severe stroke, end-stage renal [kidney] disease requiring dialysis, severe Parkinson's disease, or terminal cancer."[2]

Schizophrenia's economic costs parallel the personal disability it imposes. Schizophrenia-related costs total $80 billion to $100 billion per year in the United States alone. This includes costs for medical expenses, Social Security payments to those who are disabled, costs for families who care for schizophrenics, and criminal-justice-related costs. Most of these costs are borne by taxpayers, since few people with schizophrenia have private medical insurance. The costs in other countries are comparable. Indeed, a widely cited 2002 study in Australia found that schizophrenia-associated costs were six times greater than the total medical costs of people who have heart attacks, even though heart attacks affect twelve times more people than schizophrenia does. More recent studies worldwide show similar cost comparisons.

> "[Schizophrenia is] among the most disabling of all medical conditions."[2]
>
> —Psychiatrist Mark Olfson of Columbia University.

Roots of the Burden

Experts state that schizophrenia's immense social and economic burden stems from the fact that deinstitutionalization—a massive drive to release hundreds of thousands of severely mentally ill people from psychiatric hospitals starting in the 1960s and continuing today—backfired. Prior to the invention of the first effective treatment drugs for schizophrenia in the 1950s, most schizophrenics were confined to mental hospitals. But in the 1960s, after these medications relieved

The deinstitutionalization movement, which led to the release of hundreds of thousands of people with severe mental illness from psychiatric hospitals, also resulted in a rise in homelessness. Up to 50 percent of these patients became homeless within six months of their release.

many patients' symptoms, governments and mental health experts hoped community-based outpatient clinics would take over ongoing patient care and help severely mentally ill people be integrated into society.

Around the same time, exposés about horrific conditions and patient mistreatment in mental hospitals helped jump-start deinstitutionalization, as did a 1961 book titled *The Myth of Mental Illness* by psychiatrist Thomas Szasz. Szasz's book started the antipsychiatry movement, which blamed psychiatrists (doctors who specialize in mental illnesses) for labeling people who are "different" as mentally ill. Szasz also encouraged mentally ill people to stop taking their medications. Along with these events came laws designed to protect mentally ill people's rights. These laws made it difficult for families and law enforcement personnel to forcibly commit mentally ill people to mental hospitals or involuntarily medicate them unless they posed an immediate danger to themselves or others.

No one foresaw that these efforts to help the mentally ill would backfire, but they did because few community resources were actually implemented. Left to themselves, many patients stopped taking their medications. "The discharge of hundreds of thousands of mental patients from state hospitals was a broadly humane measure," explains psychiatrist Richard A. Friedman of Weill Cornell Medical College. "The egregious error was the failure to provide treatment to patients after they left the hospital. . . . Tragically, vast numbers of deinstitutionalized patients ended up in jails and prisons, in nursing homes or homeless on our streets."[3] Indeed, recent studies indicate that between 30 and 50 percent of patients released from mental hospitals become homeless within six months, and 45 to 64 percent of the people in American jails and prisons are severely mentally ill.

Possible Solutions

The situation has led mental health experts and lawmakers to seek ways of helping schizophrenics lead more independent, productive lives, while also safeguarding the public and diminishing schizophrenia's associated societal burden. To this end, several states have instituted new outpatient programs in recent years and have passed laws that allow judges to give mentally ill people who have committed crimes or are at high risk of committing crimes the option of entering these programs instead of being jailed or hospitalized. Although it is too early to assess how effective these programs will be, preliminary data indicates that patients and law enforcement departments are seeing positive results.

"Tragically, vast numbers of deinstitutionalized patients ended up in jails and prisons, in nursing homes or homeless on our streets."[3]

—Psychiatrist Richard A. Friedman of Weill Cornell Medical College.

Studies indicate that patients who partner with doctors to set up their own care plan are more likely to stay on their medications, so programs that allow patients who are coherent enough to help determine ideal treatments are also being explored. Other studies find that starting treatment soon after schizophrenia begins improves outcomes, so early treatment programs are also being implemented. Research to invent new, more effective medications is also under way.

Other efforts strive to serve the needs of a variety of patients, in response to studies like one published in 2014 in the *International Journal of Mental Health Systems*. The study noted, "The trick for governments is to find a judicious mix of community, outpatient, and inpatient services."[4] In line with these efforts, advocacy organizations like the National Alliance on Mental Illness (NAMI) are striving to diminish the stigma associated with schizophrenia in the hope that communities will be more willing to accept schizophrenics. With a combination of efforts, patients, families, and mental health advocates hope the personal and societal burden of schizophrenia will eventually be reduced.

CHAPTER 1

What Is Schizophrenia?

The NAMI describes schizophrenia as "a mental illness that interferes with a person's ability to think clearly, manage emotions, make decisions and relate to others."[5] The disease is also classified as a chronic (long-term) psychosis (a disorder that impairs patients' ability to distinguish fantasy from reality). Psychiatrists consider psychoses to be the most serious mental illnesses.

Centuries of Madness

Some experts believe schizophrenia did not become common until the 1700s, whereas others think it has affected people throughout human history. References to mental disorders described as "madness" or "demonic possession" exist in documents from ancient Mesopotamian, Egyptian, Hindu, and Chinese civilizations, as well as in Bible stories. These mental disorders all share characteristics of schizophrenia. For instance, writings on stone tablets dating from Mesopotamia around 3000 BCE describe an illness that featured the paranoid delusions (false beliefs of persecution) that occur in many schizophrenics. Similarly, according to *Scientific American*, the ancient Hindu Vedas dating from around 1400 BCE describe mental illnesses "characterized by bizarre behavior, lack of self-control, filth, and nudity brought on by devils."[6]

Documents from ancient Rome and Greece and from the Middle Ages also include references to schizophrenia-like diseases. The ancient Roman physician Caelius Aurelianus, for example, described people whose delusions led them to believe they were a god, a sparrow, an actor, or an ear of corn. Centuries later, documents from the mid-1300s described an Italian scribe who believed he could see the Virgin Mary, withdrew from others, and created odd maps.

Those who believe schizophrenia was rarely seen until the eighteenth century state that earlier references to madness were probably describing mental disorders that resulted from other causes. For example, some scholars believe that the prophet Ezekiel had hallucinations (visions or sensations that are not really present). Some experts think this indicated he had schizophrenia, while others believe he actually ingested hallucinogenic mushrooms that caused his symptoms. A 2012 article in the *Harvard Review of Psychiatry* also notes that serious mental disease before the mid-1700s "was caused by many medical conditions (e.g. brain tumors, alcoholic encephalitis, and various metabolic diseases.)"[7] Some medical historians also argue that mental diseases affecting young people and those that involve auditory (hearing) hallucinations—which are hallmarks of schizophrenia—were rarely described before the 1700s.

Dementia Praecox and Schizophrenia

Whether or not schizophrenia has existed throughout history, during the 1700s and 1800s doctors' descriptions of cases that were undoubtedly schizophrenia increased dramatically. Indeed, the increases were so dramatic that the first hospitals devoted strictly to mental diseases opened in many places. The first such hospital in the United States opened in Williamsburg, Virginia, in 1773.

With the increase in cases came increasingly detailed descriptions of various types and subtypes of what eventually became known as schizophrenia. In 1810 the British pharmacist John Haslam published the book *Illustrations of Madness*, in which he presented the first detailed description of what came to be called paranoid schizophrenia. Haslam described the delusional world of a patient named James Tilley Matthews, who was confined to the Bethlem mental hospital in London because he publicly accused government leaders of plotting to kill him. According to Haslam, Matthews spoke of a gang of people who assaulted him with an "Air Loom" that produced "a list of calamities hitherto unheard of," including "*Fluid-locking*, which renders Matthews speechless, *Cutting Soul From Sense*, which causes his feelings to be severed from his thoughts, and *Thigh-talking*, which produces the auditory distortion of one's ear being in one's thigh."[8]

Haslam and other experts in the early 1800s simply described people like Matthews as "mad." It was not until the late 1800s that psychiatrists described three separate diseases that were eventually labeled as subtypes of schizophrenia. The disease that involved paranoid delusions was called paranoid psychosis; one that featured disorganized behavior and speech was hebephrenia; and one characterized by immobility was named catatonia. In 1896 the German psychiatrist Emil Kraepelin grouped these three distinct disorders into a single disease he called dementia praecox, meaning dementia that occurs early in life. Kraepelin also distinguished dementia praecox from the other major psychosis, which was then known as manic-depressive illness and is now called bipolar disorder.

In 1911 the Swiss psychiatrist Eugen Bleuler coined the term *schizophrenia* to replace *dementia praecox*. Bleuler believed it was important to distinguish schizophrenia from senile dementia, which generally occurs late in life. He chose the term *schizophrenia* to describe the fragmented thinking and break with reality that characterize the disease. The word comes from the Greek terms *schizo*, meaning "split," and *phrene*, meaning "the mind." Bleuler wrote in his book *Dementia Praecox or the Group of Schizophrenias*, "I call dementia praecox 'schizophrenia' because the 'splitting' of the different psychic functions is one of its most important characteristics."[9] However, the term has been widely misinterpreted to mean a split personality, which is an entirely different disorder.

> "I call dementia praecox 'schizophrenia' because the 'splitting' of the different psychic functions is one of its most important characteristics."[9]
>
> —Swiss psychiatrist Eugen Bleuler.

Who Is Affected?

During the 1900s and early 2000s, the incidence of schizophrenia continued to grow throughout much of the world. Today the disease affects about 1 percent of the population worldwide, or more than 21 million people, according to the World Health Organization. *The Merck Manual* medical reference book for doctors states that the incidence of schizophrenia "is comparable among men and women and relatively constant cross-culturally. The rate is higher among lower

Male schizophrenics usually develop the disorder at an earlier age than females. The average age of onset for males is eighteen to twenty-five. The average age of onset for females is twenty-five to thirty-five. This graph shows how many males and females develop schizophrenia at different ages.

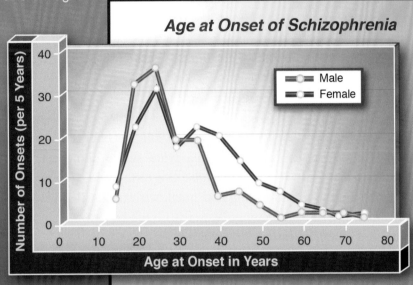

Age at Onset of Schizophrenia

Source: Appalachian State University, "Schizophrenia." www1.appstate.edu.

socioeconomic classes in urban areas, perhaps because its disabling effects lead to unemployment and poverty."[10] Experts believe about 3 million Americans currently have schizophrenia.

Although most cases of schizophrenia begin during adolescence or young adulthood, it is known to present in young children and older people. Experts call the disease childhood schizophrenia when it begins in children under thirteen and late-onset schizophrenia when it begins after age forty.

In general, men tend to develop schizophrenia earlier than women. The average age of onset for men is eighteen to twenty-five, whereas in women it is twenty-five to thirty-five. Some studies indicate that women also tend to have less severe symptoms than men, but other studies find no such trends unless the woman develops late-onset schizophrenia, which happens more often in women than in men. Overall, the earlier the disease begins, the more severe it is.

Schizophrenia Phases

Whenever schizophrenia begins, it features several characteristic phases in most patients. Doctors call the phase before the illness the premorbid phase. During this phase, according to *The Merck Manual*, "patients may show no symptoms or may have impaired social competence, mild cognitive disorganization or perceptual distortions, a diminished capacity to experience pleasure (anhedonia), and other general coping deficiencies."[11]

After the premorbid phase, most cases start gradually, with symptoms and odd behaviors emerging over several years during the prodromal phase. During this phase the individual often starts to withdraw socially, has difficulty sleeping, becomes irritable, has increasingly distorted sensory experiences, and behaves in ways that lead to a drop in grades in school or in performance at a job. For instance, in her book *Ben Behind His Voices*, Randye Kaye describes how her son gradually changed from being an outgoing child and a top student to being an angry adolescent who could not pay attention in school, refused to do his homework, drank alcohol and smoked marijuana, defied her house rules, stopped showering, ran away from home, and wrote cryptic poetry before developing full-blown schizophrenia.

Doctors have long known that it is often difficult to distinguish the prodromal phase from the premorbid phase; indeed, these phases often overlap. For example, in 1919 Kraepelin wrote that "in a considerable number of cases definite *psychic peculiarities* have come under observation in our patients from childhood up . . . many years before the real onset of dementia praecox."[12] In one of the most extreme cases ever reported, the parents of Jani Schofield, who was diagnosed with schizophrenia in 2008 at age five, told reporters they knew something was very wrong with Jani from the time of her birth. As an infant, she only slept for a few minutes at a time, for a maximum of four hours per day (most babies sleep up to sixteen hours per day). By age two she was scratching and biting her parents and baby brother because

Schizophrenia and the Bible

Experts who believe schizophrenia has existed throughout human history cite several biblical accounts of mental illnesses they believe closely resemble the disease. For example, the story of Nebuchadnezzar in the book of Daniel states that Nebuchadnezzar "was driven from men, and did eat grass as oxen." Some medical historians have interpreted this to represent the odd behaviors and social rejection that characterize schizophrenia.

Biblical scholars also note that the book of Ezekiel describes the prophet Ezekiel hearing the voice of God ninety-three times, far more often than any other prophet, which suggests that he had auditory hallucinations. Ezekiel also experienced others types of hallucinations in which he described meeting extraterrestrial beings and seeing a huge cloud that flashed with fire and "in the middle of it was something like four living creatures. . . . Each had four faces, and each of them had four wings."

Other experts believe these stories may have involved conditions other than schizophrenia. The book *Your Brain on Food*, for instance, states:

> The widespread use of hallucinogenic plants by our ancestors may underlie some of the fantastic stories that have become associated with various religions. For example, some people believe the Book of Ezekiel describes this prophet's encounter with beings from outer space during the sixth century BCE; a more reasonable explanation might be that the experience was initiated by the consumption of an hallucinogenic plant.

Daniel 4:33, King James Bible, Cambridge Edition.

Ezekiel 1:5–6, New Revised Standard Version, Anglicized Catholic Edition.

Gary L. Wenk, *Your Brain on Food*. New York: Oxford University Press, 2015, p. 136.

imaginary creatures told her to do so. By age five she kept trying to choke herself and tried to jump from a window.

Whether or not the premorbid and prodromal phases overlap, the middle phase follows the prodromal phase. During the middle phase, some patients have continuous psychotic symptoms and others have discrete psychotic episodes, after which they may appear to recover for some length of time. Overall functioning deteriorates during this phase, and the individual often becomes unable or unwilling to care for him- or herself. During the next stage, the late phase, the person's pattern of psychotic episodes becomes established, but there are wide variations in whether the level of disability stabilizes, becomes better, or worsens.

In each phase symptoms vary widely among individuals. Until recently psychiatrists used an individual's most prominent symptoms to categorize the disease into the subtypes of paranoid, catatonic, disorganized, undifferentiated, or residual schizophrenia. Today these categories have been removed from the fifth edition of the *Diagnostic and Statistical Manual of Mental Disorders* (DSM-5), the manual psychiatrists use to diagnose mental diseases.

The emphasis is now on whether an individual's symptoms are positive or negative. These descriptions do not refer to whether a symptom is good or bad, but rather if it constitutes added or enhanced cognitive, emotional, and behavioral qualities (positive) or reduced or deficient ones (negative). The positive and negative categories now used to help diagnose schizophrenia are useful in predicting disease progression and the probability of successful treatment. Patients with negative symptoms have the worst disease progression and the least chance of being helped by treatment.

Since many symptoms, both positive and negative, involve distorted thinking and a loss of cognitive capabilities, some experts include cognitive symptoms in descriptions of these categories. Some, however, refer to cognitive symptoms as a separate category.

Positive Symptoms

Positive symptoms include delusions, hallucinations, a distorted sense of self, and unusual sensations that highlight the patient's psychotic break with reality. Delusions and hallucinations are among the most obvious positive symptoms. The most common type of hallucinations are auditory. Patients may hear one or more voices that comment on their behavior, tell them to do things, or warn them about things that are about to happen. For example, a schizophrenic named Alita Van Hee told the *New York Times* that voices "would tell me things like 'Don't trust these people,' 'Don't talk to your friends,' things like that.

It's kind of like having a TV or radio on blasting inside your head just all the time that you can't turn off no matter what you do."[13]

Delusions vary widely, too, but often derive from situations in which schizophrenics find themselves. For instance, if schizophrenics see a helicopter in the sky, they may believe it is spying on them or trying to kill them. Later, if they see someone sneeze, they may believe the sneeze is part of the plot. Doctors and others who interact with schizophrenics say it is futile to try to reason with a schizophrenic about the falseness of such delusions, since the individual is so convinced they are real.

> "It's kind of like having a TV or radio on blasting inside your head just all the time that you can't turn off no matter what you do."[13]
>
> —Schizophrenia patient Alita Van Hee.

Delusions are often prominent in children with schizophrenia. These delusions are usually age appropriate; some children imagine that monsters are coming to get them or that toys are talking to them. Many children's delusions involve family members. One mother stated that her son "would call me by a name that no one understood, he said I was from a different planet sent here to kill him. He told his siblings they were from his planet and they were here to protect him."[14]

Another common type of positive symptom involves a distorted sense of self. A 2012 study published in the *Schizophrenia Bulletin* explains that schizophrenics "experience one's body as an object rather than an 'inhabited' aspect of selfhood."[15] Some patients report that an arm or leg feels foreign or like it is not in its correct place. Others cannot distinguish their own body from other people's bodies. One woman was unsure of where her body ended and that of her mother began.

This distorted sense of self often goes hand in hand with another characteristic symptom in which patients believe their thoughts are being spoken aloud or that others can read their thoughts. Experts call this symptom thought broadcasting. For example, in his book *Recovered, Not Cured*, a schizophrenic named Richard McLean writes, "I was really upset the other night because the people on the news were saying what my thoughts were. I know this is true because they

Children with schizophrenia often experience delusions. Sometimes they think their toys are talking to them or that monsters are after them.

sent me messages on what they were doing."[16] Indeed, many radio and television stations report that schizophrenics visit them and demand that the station stop broadcasting their thoughts.

Negative Symptoms

Negative symptoms are less obvious than positive ones, but they are just as disturbing to patients and observers. Common negative symptoms are a decrease or loss of the ability to pay attention, understand things, remember, speak coherently, express or feel emotions (known as blunted emotions), and find joy in life. The emotional distortions patients experience also lead them to express inappropriate emotions— for instance, laughing when a friend dies. Lack of self-care and lack of awareness of one's illness are other common negative symptoms. Psychiatrists call this lack of awareness *anosognosia*, meaning "no disease knowledge" in Greek. It occurs in about 60 percent of patients. As the NAMI explains, anosognosia "is not a conscious choice

"I was really upset the other night because the people on the news were saying what my thoughts were. I know this is true because they sent me messages on what they were doing."[16]

—Schizophrenia patient Richard McLean.

to misattribute, or deny, the symptoms but rather a symptom of the illness itself."[17] As with delusions, people with anosognosia do not change their beliefs when confronted with overwhelming evidence that they are sick.

Negative symptoms also involve a lack of organized thoughts and speech. Schizophrenics often link unrelated things together, a phenomenon known as loose associations. For example, an individual may say, "Hamburger mountain time sleep." Kraepelin described this prominent feature by stating that patients' minds suffer a "loss of inner unity" and operate like an "orchestra without a conductor."[18]

Other Symptoms

Many patients report that their mental and emotional symptoms stem from an overwhelming onslaught of sensations that leave them confused and frightened. Whereas most people's minds screen or filter incoming sights and other sensations so they can concentrate, schizophrenics lack this ability and thus cannot focus their thoughts.

About two-thirds of patients also report experiencing altered sensations, which may include changes in vision, hearing, taste, smell, or touch. In some people sensations are diminished, particularly during the middle and late phases of the disease. That is, noises may sound unusually soft or colors may seem dull. One woman stated, "Everything tastes like sawdust."[19] Others experience a diminished sense of touch to the extent that they do not feel physical pain. A 2010 report by doctors at Hirosaki University in Japan described a female patient who had a ruptured appendix, which is typically very painful, yet she did not appear to feel any pain. The doctors noted that a lack of pain often results in serious diseases or injuries advancing to the point that they cause a patient's death.

Other schizophrenics, however, experience heightened sensations. This most often happens early in the disease. One man, for instance, described how he felt like he was being electrocuted every time someone touched him. One woman stated, "I saw the colors of the grass, flowers, and sky as sharper, more vivid. Reds, yellows, and oranges actually hurt my eyes."[20] In some people these heightened sensations underlie delusions of grandeur, in which individuals believe their newfound ability to see things sharply gives them godlike powers.

Along with these characteristic mental symptoms come behavioral changes such as moving very slowly or quickly. Many schizophrenics develop repetitive movements such as constant blinking, twitching body parts, lip smacking, or odd tongue movements. On rare occasions patients become catatonic and do not move at all, sometimes for months. Psychiatrists believe such behaviors are a re-

Reasons for New Diagnostic Criteria

In 2013 the American Psychiatric Association adopted the fifth edition of the *Diagnostic and Statistical Manual of Mental Disorders*, which did away with the five traditional subtypes of schizophrenia (paranoid, disorganized, catatonic, undifferentiated, and residual) because experts found these to be unreliable methods of assessing patients. According to the DSM-5, the subtypes "were not helpful to clinicians because patients' symptoms often changed from one subtype to another and presented overlapping subtype symptoms, which blurred distinctions among the five subtypes and decreased their validity." Psychiatrists also found that these subtypes were not useful in predicting the outcome of the disease in most patients. In addition, experts noted that very few schizophrenics exhibit catatonic symptoms. A 2010 article in the *Schizophrenia Bulletin*, for instance, states that catatonia is seen much more often in people with mania, depression, and various neurological diseases and thus should not be considered a subtype of schizophrenia.

Although several psychiatrists have proposed new subtypes such as nondeficit and deficit schizophrenia (based on the positive and negative symptom categories used in DSM-5), no new subtypes have yet been adopted.

American Psychiatric Association, "Schizophrenia." www.dsm5.org.

sponse to the overwhelming confusion brought about by sensory and cognitive changes. In a similar manner, behavior that involves substance abuse is also common; it often stems from an attempt to escape from disturbing symptoms.

Difficulties in Diagnosis

Given the wide variety and severity of behavioral and cognitive symptoms, it is often difficult for doctors to diagnose schizophrenia. Diagnostic difficulties also arise because no single laboratory or brain imaging test can diagnose the disease. Doctors diagnose most diseases by measuring certain objective qualities, such as the presence of cancer cells or cholesterol in the blood. But no such measurable features clearly define schizophrenia. Psychiatrists hope that someday objective blood or brain imaging tests will diagnose schizophrenia, but no such tools exist today.

The fact that other brain disorders—such as brain tumors or brain damage from illegal drug use—can cause symptoms similar to schizophrenia also makes it difficult to diagnose the disease. Doctors make a diagnosis based on subjective assessments of symptoms over time, along with using blood tests and imaging tests such as computed tomography (CT) or magnetic resonance imaging (MRI) to rule out other brain diseases. CT uses computerized X-rays, and MRI uses radio waves and magnets to view internal structures. Studies indicate that it can take up to ten years to correctly diagnose schizophrenia.

Making a correct diagnosis in adolescents is especially difficult because many teenagers act out or rebel, experiment with alcohol and drugs, express anger at their parents, or neglect their studies. Randye Kaye revealed that it took more than six years and several hospitalizations before doctors correctly diagnosed her son, because she, his school counselors, and his doctors were unsure whether his behaviors were typical teenaged ones or indicated something more serious. Before being diagnosed with schizophrenia, he was wrongly diagnosed with attention-deficit/hyperactivity disorder, substance abuse, bipolar disorder, anxiety disorder, and obsessive-compulsive disorder.

Diagnosing people with late-onset schizophrenia is also especially difficult because the incidence of senile dementia and similar dis-

Diagnosing schizophrenia in teenagers can be difficult. Many common teen behaviors such as acting out, experimenting with drugs and alcohol, and expressing anger toward parents can also be signs of a variety of mental disorders including schizophrenia.

orders increases with age. According to researchers at the University of California–San Diego, doctors evaluating older patients with psychotic symptoms "should keep in mind that a condition other than schizophrenia may be the cause. Psychosis of Alzheimer's disease is common in this population—as many as half of all patients with Alzheimer's disease develop psychotic symptoms."[21]

Diagnostic Criteria

Since early diagnosis can positively influence the chances for successful treatment and recovery, experts are working to develop predictive criteria that allow doctors to accurately state which early signs, such as altered sensations, are likely to lead to full-blown schizophrenia. Doctors also look for symptoms that rarely occur in diseases other than schizophrenia to help make diagnosis easier. Such symptoms include auditory hallucinations, thought broadcasting, and a distorted sense of self.

Even when patients have symptoms that overlap with other diseases, psychiatrists find that assessing the number and duration of schizophrenia-related symptoms is the most reliable diagnostic method thus far. Diagnostic criteria listed in the DSM-5, adopted in 2013, include the presence of two or more symptoms from a list that includes delusions, hallucinations, disorganized speech, catatonia or other abnormal movements, lack of emotion, lack of the ability to converse with others, decreased function at school or work, and lack of self-care. At least one symptom must be a positive symptom experienced for a significant amount of time over one or more thirty-day periods that have recurred for at least six months. Other conditions, including substance abuse, that could account for a patient's symptoms must also be ruled out.

If symptoms have not continued for at least six months, psychiatrists usually diagnose schizophreniform disorder if they suspect that schizophrenia will be diagnosed eventually. Schizophreniform disorder is thus a disorder that serves as a preliminary diagnosis of schizophrenia in people who have not yet satisfied the criteria for being diagnosed as schizophrenic.

There are also diseases that are similar to schizophrenia but less severe. The DSM-5 specifies that schizophrenia and these related disorders fall on a spectrum. At one end of the spectrum is full-blown schizophrenia, with other conditions like schizoaffective disorder and schizotypal personality disorder elsewhere on the spectrum. Schizoaffective disorder includes symptoms of both schizophrenia and bipolar disorder. Schizophrenia primarily involves thought abnormalities, and bipolar disorder primarily involves emotional abnormalities. Schizotypal personality disorder is a relatively mild form of schizophrenia; it applies to people with typical schizophrenia symptoms but whose lives are not disrupted to a great extent. Researchers have determined that the range of severity and symptoms in different people result from a variety of biological and environmental factors.

CHAPTER 2

What Causes Schizophrenia?

Throughout history, most people believed mental illnesses such as schizophrenia were caused by demonic possession. But in the late 1800s, Emil Kraepelin and other experts proposed that schizophrenia was caused by genetic and other biological factors. Kraepelin wrote it was likely "that what we have here is a tangible morbid process in the brain."[22]

However, during the first half of the 1900s, biological theories were sidelined when the Austrian neurologist Sigmund Freud's psychoanalytic theories dominated the field of psychiatry, and related biological research slowed considerably. Psychoanalysis emphasized the role of parents and early life experiences in causing mental diseases, and most doctors during this era thought bad parenting caused schizophrenia. Biological theories again became prominent during the late 1900s, and experts today have established that abnormalities in brain structure and function cause schizophrenia. As psychiatrist E. Fuller Torrey writes in his book *Surviving Schizophrenia*, "We now clearly understand that schizophrenia is a disease of the brain, nothing more and nothing less."[23] These brain abnormalities, in turn, result from complex interactions between genes and a variety of environmental factors.

The Human Brain

The brain is part of the central nervous system, which consists of the brain and spinal cord. The entire nervous system is made up of the central nervous system and the peripheral nervous system, which consists of nerve fibers that extend from the spinal cord to organs and other body parts.

As the body's command center, the brain is well protected. It lies inside protective bones known as the skull and is surrounded by fluid called cerebrospinal fluid. This fluid also flows through four canals called ventricles in the brain's center. Biologists divide the brain's structure into two halves, or hemispheres, and four main sections called lobes—the frontal, parietal, temporal, and occipital lobes. There is much overlap in what these parts of the brain do, but the cortex (outer section) of the frontal lobe primarily regulates intellectual functions, language, personality, and some motor functions. The parietal lobe mostly processes sensory information. The temporal lobe mostly regulates hearing and language, and the occipital lobe primarily regulates vision. Under the lobes are the limbic system, which plays a big role in emotions and memory, and the cerebellum, which regulates movement.

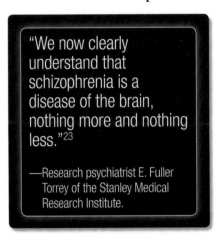

"We now clearly understand that schizophrenia is a disease of the brain, nothing more and nothing less."[23]

—Research psychiatrist E. Fuller Torrey of the Stanley Medical Research Institute.

The various parts of the brain function and communicate through more than 100 billion neurons (nerve cells) and other cells, such as glial cells, which support neurons by providing nourishment and other necessities. Neurons consist of a cell body, long extensions called axons, and short extensions called dendrites. The cell body contains the nucleus that houses the cell's genetic material and tiny organs that conduct cell operations. Axons transmit messages to other neurons using chemical and electrical signals. Dendrites contain receptors that receive these messages. The average neuron in the human brain receives input from one to ten thousand other neurons.

The main means of communication between neurons involves neurotransmitters, or brain chemicals. Scientists have identified more than one hundred different neurotransmitters; some of the best known are dopamine, acetylcholine, serotonin, and glutamate. When a neurotransmitter reaches another cell's dendrites, this causes the receiving neuron to release an electrical impulse that prompts that neuron to release its own neurotransmitters. Neurons release and receive neurotransmitters across a tiny gap (about one-millionth of an inch wide) known as a synapse. Neurons in one part of the brain also communicate with other brain areas using these chemical signals. As the book *Diagnosis: Schizophrenia* explains, "The brain is like the Internet. Signals get sent and are received among many parts of a complicated system."[24]

Brain Abnormalities

Scientists study the structure of the brain by dissecting the brains of deceased people and by using CT or MRI to generate images of internal structures. They study brain activity using technologies such as functional MRI (fMRI), which measures blood flow in various areas. Studies of brain structure and function in schizophrenics indicate that many brain areas and their interconnections are abnormal.

In the late 1970s CT scans provided the first real evidence that brain abnormalities might cause schizophrenia. Scientists discovered that many schizophrenics' ventricles are about 15 percent larger than normal. Later studies found that many schizophrenics' brains are smaller and have abnormal cell structure in areas like the frontal lobe, hippocampus, amygdala, parahippocampal gyrus, and cingulate.

Some research indicates that more severe cases of schizophrenia are accompanied by greater structural abnormalities. For example, a 2012 study in *Current Psychiatry Reports* found that people with full-blown schizophrenia have much more extensive size reductions in the frontal lobe than those who have the less severe schizotypal personality disorder (SPD). The researchers wrote that "larger frontal lobe volume in SPD may serve to protect these individuals from the full-blown psychosis seen in schizophrenia."[25] However, other studies indicate that smaller size and enlarged ventricles do not seem to influence symptom severity. A 2014 study in Finland, for instance, concluded, "Symptom severity, functioning level, and decline in cognition were not associated with brain volume reduction in schizophrenia."[26] Researchers are currently studying exactly how these structural abnormalities affect the disease.

Although the effects of structural abnormalities are unclear, scientists do know that abnormal brain activity in certain areas causes schizophrenia's characteristic symptoms. For instance, schizophrenics' brains show abnormal neuron activity in the temporoparietal

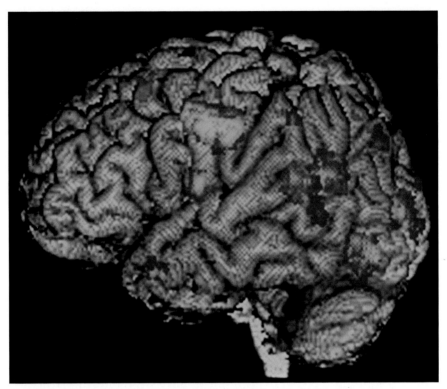

Scientists often use brain imaging to study schizophrenia. Pictured are areas of activity (orange) in the brain of a schizophrenia patient who is experiencing hallucinations. The colored regions control visual and auditory functions.

junction and superior temporal gyrus, which are involved in hearing. Experts believe these abnormalities are responsible for auditory hallucinations. Other studies indicate that abnormal activity in the inferior parietal lobule underlies delusions in which schizophrenics believe they are being controlled by others. Still other research links abnormal activity in the dorsolateral prefrontal cortex and temporal cortex to negative symptoms.

Neuron and Communication Abnormalities

Researchers also find abnormalities in neurons, the glial cells that support neurons, and neurotransmitters in schizophrenics' brains. Sometimes, neurons have too many or too few receptors, or there might be too many or too few neurons releasing certain neurotransmitters. In these cases signals become garbled, which can lead to hallucinations, delusions, or disorganized speech. Studies show that abnormalities in the release or uptake of the neurotransmitters dopamine, acetylcholine, serotonin, noradrenalin, glutamate, and gamma-aminobutyric acid (GABA) play a role in causing such symptoms.

The role of dopamine has been studied the most extensively, since some studies show that schizophrenics have excess dopamine in various brain areas. As a result, most drugs used to treat schizophrenia block dopamine. Some newer treatment drugs, however, do not have much effect on dopamine, so experts have concluded that other neurotransmitters must play a role in causing symptoms as well. For example, a 2010 study reported in the journal *Lancet* stated that issues with serotonin, glutamate, and natural opioids (all neurotransmitters) could account for why some schizophrenics do not feel pain.

Other research indicates that malfunctions in the dorsolateral prefrontal cortex, which is important in memory formation, result from having too few neurochemicals that regulate GABA and from having abnormal receptors in neurons that take up GABA. GABA's primary role is to slow brain activity. It is believed these malfunctions affect how the dorsolateral prefrontal cortex processes information and could be the reason why schizophrenics have various memory problems.

Other brain chemicals called neuropeptides, such as somatostatin and neurotensin, also influence schizophrenia, since these protein-like substances affect neurotransmitters. Neurons release neuropeptides to help them communicate with other neurons. For example, areas of the brain that produce and respond to dopamine release large amounts of neurotensin, which changes the rate at which dopamine neurons fire. Many schizophrenics have abnormally low amounts of neurotensin in their cerebrospinal fluid, and studies indicate that people with the least amount of neurotensin have the worst symptoms.

Genetics and Schizophrenia

The underlying causes of these structural and functional brain abnormalities involve both genetic and environmental factors. Experts have known for years that schizophrenia runs in families. In fact, having a close relative with schizophrenia is the greatest known risk factor for developing it. According to the National Institute of Mental Health (NIMH):

> The illness occurs in 1 percent of the general population, but it occurs in 10 percent of people who have a first-degree relative with the disorder, such as a parent, brother, or sister. People who have second-degree relatives (aunts, uncles, grandparents, or cousins) with the disease also develop schizophrenia more often than the general population. The risk is highest for an identical twin of a person with schizophrenia. He or she has a 40 to 65 percent chance of developing the disorder.[27]

The reason family members are at high risk is that they share many genes. Identical twins, in fact, have identical genes. Genes are the parts of deoxyribonucleic acid (DNA) molecules that transmit hereditary information from parents to their offspring. Genes instruct cells how to operate. The human genome (the complete set of genes)

Experts have long known that schizophrenia runs in families. The risk is especially high for identical twins; when one twin is diagnosed with schizophrenia the other twin has a high likelihood of also developing the disorder.

consists of about twenty-two thousand genes. These are housed on twenty-three pairs of chromosomes. Humans inherit chromosomes in pairs; one set comes from each parent. Changes, or mutations, can occur in genes while they are being copied from parents' DNA, while a fetus is developing, or after birth, due to damage from environmental factors such as radiation or viruses.

Even tiny changes in the nucleotides (chemical building blocks) that make up DNA can influence susceptibility to certain diseases.

Unlike some diseases that are caused by a single abnormal gene, scientists have found that people can inherit a predisposition to schizophrenia, rather than inheriting the disease itself. Such a predisposition results from a variety (perhaps hundreds) of gene abnormalities. Scientists have not yet identified all the responsible genes but have tied many to the disease. For instance, a 2014 study conducted at dozens of international research institutions and reported in the journal *Nature* found 108 places in the human genome related to the risk of developing schizophrenia.

> "The illness occurs in 1 percent of the general population, but it occurs in 10 percent of people who have a first-degree relative with the disorder, such as a parent, brother, or sister."[27]
>
> —The NIMH.

Mutations and Schizophrenia

Some gene abnormalities related to schizophrenia disrupt brain development and functioning by causing neurons to produce abnormal amounts of certain neurotransmitters. Some lead to abnormalities in the way dendrite receptors take up neurotransmitters. For example, a 2011 University of Pittsburgh study tied abnormal GABA activity in the dorsolateral prefrontal cortex to memory impairments. The study found that the genes reelin, parvalbumin, and GAD 67, which govern GABA activity, are consistently abnormal in schizophrenics. These gene abnormalities lead neurons to produce less-than-normal amounts of chemicals that regulate the release and uptake of GABA.

Other research indicates that abnormalities in the catechol-O-methyltransferase gene, which regulates activity in the prefrontal cortex, also appear consistently in schizophrenics. Another common

The First Evidence for a Genetic Cause of Schizophrenia

Psychiatrist Seymour S. Kety of Harvard University was the first doctor to provide strong evidence that genes play a role in causing schizophrenia. Kety and a group of Danish researchers used national birth registries in Denmark to track schizophrenia in people who were separated from their biological families at birth and adopted. As Kety explained in 1976 in a *Behavior Genetics* article, "Since an adopted individual receives his genetic endowment from one family and his life experience as a member of another it may be possible to disentangle genetic and environmental factors by studies based on such individuals and their biological and adoptive families."

Kety's research showed that 10 percent of the biological relatives of schizophrenics who were adopted had the disease themselves—a fivefold increase over the incidence of schizophrenia in the general population. The adoptive relatives of schizophrenics did not have schizophrenia more often than people in the general population. Furthermore, children born to a schizophrenic mother and raised in an adoptive home developed schizophrenia as often as children born to a schizophrenic mother and reared in her home. This provided compelling evidence that genes are an important cause of the disease.

Seymour S. Kety et al., "Mental Illness in the Biological and Adoptive Families of Adopted Individuals Who Have Become Schizophrenic," *Behavior Genetics*, vol. 6, no. 3, 1976, p. 220.

mutation appears in the metabotropic glutamate receptor 3 gene, which regulates glutamate. In 2011 researchers at the University of California–San Diego identified yet another gene mutation that generated excitement in the research community because it is rarely found in diseases other than schizophrenia. They discovered that many people with schizophrenia have extra copies of the Viper 2 gene located on chromosome 7. Viper 2 regulates the development of the nervous system before birth.

Scientists have discovered that many gene mutations that consistently appear in schizophrenics result from single nucleotide polymorphisms (SNPs). SNPs are minor changes in the normal biochemical structure of genes. The human body uses the nucleotides adenine (A), guanine (G), cytosine (C), and thymine (T) to create DNA. If the normal structure of a particular gene is, say, AGTCCGT, an SNP might replace one nucleotide, with the end product being AGTCCAT. SNPs can also involve nucleotide deletions. Any SNP can alter how the gene is expressed (how cells follow the gene's instructions). Research indicates the neuron abnormalities that result from schizophrenia-related SNPs often cause these neurons to respond abnormally to certain environmental events.

Gene-Environment Interactions

Researchers know that although genes play a big role in whether a person is susceptible to schizophrenia, complex gene-environment interactions underlie the brain abnormalities that cause the disease. If genes were the only factors involved, then 100 percent of identical twins affected by schizophrenia would both have the disease. However, only 40 to 65 percent of identical twins are both affected.

One prominent theory about how these gene-environment interactions work is the neurodevelopmental theory. This theory states that gene mutations and environmental events lead to problems with brain development before birth, which results in abnormal brain structure and neural connections that usually have little or no effect until puberty. Then hormonal changes and other changes that occur during puberty somehow trigger psychotic symptoms. Although experts are unsure of exactly which environmental factors are critical, studies indicate that birth complications, viruses and other pathogens, street drug use, age of the father when the child is born, and possibly other factors play a role.

Environmental Triggers

Numerous studies indicate that children born to fathers over age forty are at increased risk of developing schizophrenia. However, a 2013 study reported in the journal *Cell* suggests that this can happen when fathers are as young as thirty-three. The study also sheds light on the processes involved. It found that schizophrenics whose fathers were thirty-three to forty-five years old when the child was conceived were much more likely to have spontaneous mutations in fifty-four genes than schizophrenics whose fathers were nineteen to twenty-eight at conception. Spontaneous mutations are DNA changes that occur after conception. Most of the fifty-four mutated genes cause abnormal proteins to be produced in the prefrontal cortex. These proteins damage the brain during fetal development. Researchers believe this contributes to the later development of schizophrenia.

Another factor known to increase the risk of schizophrenia is the use of street drugs such as marijuana, LSD, and methamphetamine. One of the most-studied such drugs is marijuana. Numerous studies indicate that smoking marijuana significantly increases the risk of developing schizophrenia. The more an individual uses marijuana, the greater the risk, and the earlier the person is likely to develop schizophrenia. A 2011 study showed that people with mutations in a gene called AKT1 were the most likely to suffer brain damage from the toxic effects of marijuana and were most likely to develop psychosis after using the drug. However, even though street drugs damage the brain, E. Fuller Torrey writes, "There is virtually no evidence . . . that the use of these drugs can actually *cause* schizophrenia in a person who is not already in the process of getting it."[28]

The role of birth complications has also been widely studied. Research indicates that being deprived of oxygen during birth often leads to the type of brain damage that causes schizophrenia. Studies on rat pups suggest why this may occur. These studies indicate that the brains of animals deprived of oxygen during birth have abnormally high amounts of dopamine in areas linked to schizophrenia.

Infections and Schizophrenia

One of the most-studied types of environmental events linked to triggering schizophrenia in genetically susceptible individuals is exposure to viruses and other pathogens before birth. For example, researchers found that children born to mothers infected by influenza viruses in the second month of pregnancy during the 1957 influenza epidemic had double the normal risk of developing schizophrenia. A 2004 study found that children exposed to influenza in the womb during the first trimester of pregnancy were seven times more likely to

Drug use can heighten the risk of schizophrenia in a person who is genetically predisposed to developing the disorder. Researchers have identified marijuana as one of the drugs that can have this effect.

develop schizophrenia. However, some studies find no such increased risks. At the same time, other studies find that many schizophrenics have abnormally high numbers of antibodies to viruses such as herpes simplex, influenza, and Epstein-Barr, as well as to the parasite *Toxoplasma gondii*. Antibodies are chemicals the immune system produces to fight specific antigens (foreign organisms or substances) that get into the body.

Although no one has proved that these infections cause schizophrenia, several scientists have proposed that the infections activate genes that produce proteins that damage the brain in susceptible people. Research shows that *Toxoplasma gondii* and influenza virus both activate a type of gene called a human endogenous retrovirus-W (HERV-W) gene. This leads the body to produce proteins called HERV-W envelope proteins. These proteins inflame and poison the brain in areas that are abnormal in schizophrenia. According to an article in the *World Journal of Biological Psychiatry*, "HERV-W may be an important genetic factor interplaying with the environmental risk factor of infection"[29] that leads to schizophrenia.

Although numerous pathogens are linked to schizophrenia, *Toxoplasma gondii*, which is transmitted through cat feces and soil, is one of the most studied. Several researchers have written extensively about their belief that infections with this parasite may have contributed to the vast increases in cases of schizophrenia starting in the 1700s, when it became popular to keep cats as pets. Many studies also indicate that pregnant women and people with impaired immune systems are very susceptible to harm from *T. gondii*. Pregnant women can transmit the parasite to a fetus, causing brain damage or death in the fetus. This is why doctors advise pregnant women not to clean litter boxes.

T. gondii can also infect people after birth, but usually healthy people have no symptoms or mild flu-like symptoms. In fact, the Centers for Disease Control and Prevention estimates that more than 60 million people in the United States are infected, but few have symptoms. Even after an individual fights off the parasite, recent evidence suggests that it can remain dormant in brain cells and later trigger schizophrenia in genetically susceptible people.

Stress and Schizophrenia

Other recent research on environmental factors provides evidence that early life stress may trigger schizophrenia in genetically susceptible individuals. This research is controversial; indeed, some experts note that Freud's theory about bad parenting causing the disease was disproved long ago. However, a widely cited 1998 study by researchers at McGill University in Canada spurred other studies that indicate that the way parents, especially mothers, treat their babies can influence the risk of schizophrenia.

The McGill study found that the number and activity of several types of brain chemical receptors in baby rats whose mothers were nurturing—grooming and licking the babies and allowing them to nurse—differed from those in babies whose mothers were not nurturing. Baby rats with nurturing mothers also displayed less fear to stressful situations later on. The researchers concluded that "these

Cats and Schizophrenia

The Czech evolutionary biologist Jaroslav Flegr has published numerous studies linking schizophrenia to *Toxoplasma gondii*, which is transmitted through cat feces and soil. Flegr believes this parasite changes connections between neurons in the brain. However, until recently many scientists ridiculed his views, in part because Flegr himself is infected with *T. gondii* and believes the infection accounts for some of his own odd behaviors. In a 2012 article in the *Atlantic*, Flegr explained another reason for scientists' reluctance to accept his findings: "There is strong psychological resistance to the possibility that human behavior can be influenced by some stupid parasite. Nobody likes to feel like a puppet. Reviewers of my scientific papers may have been offended."

However, new independent research supports Flegr's view that *T. gondii* may trigger schizophrenia in genetically susceptible people. Researchers at Stanford University have determined that *T. gondii* does indeed rewire brain circuits that govern fear and anxiety. Other research shows that *T. gondii* manufactures dopamine and that infecting laboratory animals with the parasite leads to abnormal behavior. Furthermore, a 2014 study by professor Gary Smith at the University of Pennsylvania indicates that 20 percent of schizophrenia cases involve *T. gondii*. "If you could stop infections with this parasite," said Smith in the newspaper *Daily Mail*, "over a lifetime, we found that you could prevent one-fifth of all cases." Smith also notes that the incidence of schizophrenia is highest in countries with the most *T. gondii* infections.

Quoted in Kathleen McAuliffe, "How Your Cat Is Making You Crazy," *Atlantic*, March 2012. www.theatlantic.com.

Quoted in Sarah Griffiths, "Can You Catch Schizophrenia? Parasite Transmitted by Soil and Cat Faeces May Cause a FIFTH of Cases, Study Claims," *Daily Mail* (London), October 30, 2014. www.dailymail.co.uk.

findings suggest that maternal care during infancy serves to 'program' behavioral responses to stress in the offspring by altering the development of the neural systems that mediate fearfulness."[30]

More recent studies in humans support these findings by showing that early childhood experiences alter the development of brain structures, such as the hippocampus, that regulate people's responses to stress. These studies show that stressful experiences raise the body's level of stress hormones such as glucocorticoids, and glucocorticoids kill neurons in the hippocampus and other brain areas involved in emotions, learning, memory, and behavior. Excess glucocorticoids are also associated with high dopamine and glutamate levels in several brain areas that contribute to schizophrenia.

> "Childhood traumatic experiences represent a prominent risk factor for the development of psychotic disorders, including schizophrenia."[31]
>
> —Psychiatrist Eugene Ruby and his colleagues at New York University School of Medicine and Columbia University.

Because of such effects, researchers at Columbia University and New York University state in a 2014 study, "Childhood traumatic experiences represent a prominent risk factor for the development of psychotic disorders, including schizophrenia."[31] However, other studies indicate that people who endure traumatic events like wars, serious illnesses, and abuse do not develop schizophrenia more often than other people. This issue, like many others about what causes schizophrenia, is not yet resolved.

CHAPTER 3

What Is It like to Live with Schizophrenia?

Living with schizophrenia is extremely challenging for affected patients and families. In the short term, accepting and getting the disease under control is difficult and often frustrating, disrupting all aspects of life to a great degree. In the long term, maintaining good control and striving to live a productive life pose ongoing challenges for those who experience some degree of recovery. According to *The Merck Manual*, "Symptoms of schizophrenia typically impair the ability to function and often markedly interfere with work, social relationships, and self-care. Unemployment, isolation, deteriorated relationships, and diminished quality of life are common outcomes."[32]

Consequences of Mental Confusion

Many challenges in living and interacting with others result from patients' inability to distinguish reality from fantasy and from the onslaught of sensations that bombard their brains. Their confusion and fear prevent many schizophrenics from acting coherently and cause them to withdraw socially or behave in a frightening manner. One patient states, "An outsider may see only someone 'out of touch with reality.' In fact, we are experiencing so many realities that it is often confusing and sometimes totally overwhelming."[33]

In many cases distorted and overwhelming sensations prevent schizophrenics from following a conversation because it sounds like a foreign language when others speak. "I heard people talking, but I did not grasp the meaning of the words," explains one sufferer named Renee. "From time to time, a word detached itself from the rest. It repeated itself over and over in my head."[34]

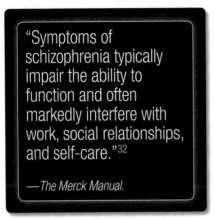

"Symptoms of schizophrenia typically impair the ability to function and often markedly interfere with work, social relationships, and self-care."[32]

—The Merck Manual.

Many schizophrenics also say that they only see parts of things or people and thus cannot recognize them. For others the mental jumble they experience prevents them from understanding what others are feeling. Therefore, if a family member or friend expresses joy or sorrow, schizophrenics will not respond at all or will respond inappropriately. Their mental confusion can also lead schizophrenics to lash out violently if they believe someone is threatening them. These types of responses feed their inability to maintain relationships and fuel their social isolation.

Stigma and Crime

The odd, fearful, or violent behaviors that result from schizophrenics' mental turmoil in turn trigger the disgust and/or fear in others that underlie the stigma and mistreatment directed at those with mental illness. Mentally ill people have been stigmatized throughout history. For instance, in ancient Rome many people believed the mentally ill were evil and should be tortured, starved, flogged, or otherwise punished.

Although most people now understand that schizophrenia is a biological disease, the stigma has not diminished; in fact, some studies show it has increased. Researchers at Palacký University in the Czech Republic explain in an article in *Neuropsychiatric Disease and Treatment* that since deinstitutionalization led many schizophrenics to live in communities, "verbal abuse and other harassment of the mentally ill by local teenagers and neighbors is . . . common."[35] The NAMI reports that about 96 percent of the schizophrenics in the United States experience prejudice or discrimination that significantly impacts their lives.

Experts say the major factor that promotes stigma is the fear that follows news stories about schizophrenics who commit violent crimes. These include James Holmes, who killed twelve people and injured dozens more in a Colorado movie theater in 2012; Jared Loughner, who killed six people and injured thirteen others, including Representative Gabrielle Giffords, near Tucson, Arizona, in 2011; and

The Stigma of Mental Illness

Although evidence shows that mental illnesses such as schizophrenia result from a brain disorder, there is still much stigma associated with this disease and with other mental disorders. Polls conducted by researchers at the Johns Hopkins Bloomberg School of Public Health in January 2013, soon after schizophrenic Adam Lanza murdered twenty-six people in Newtown, Connecticut, found that overall, nearly half of Americans believed people with serious mental illnesses are significantly more dangerous than others. More than 70 percent were unwilling to work closely on a job with someone who has a serious mental illness, and nearly 70 percent were unwilling to have a mentally ill neighbor. On some questions, opinions differed depending on the respondents' experience with mental illness.

Public Attitudes About Mental Illness

Perceived dangerousness and social distance	Overall	No Experience with Mental Illness	Experience with Mental Illness
Do you agree or disagree that people with serious mental illness are, by far, more dangerous than the general population? (% agree)	45.6%	46.3%	44.8%
Do you agree or disagree that locating a group home or apartment for people with mental illness in a residential neighborhood endangers local residents? (% agree)	31.8%	33.5%	30.1%
Would you be willing or unwilling to have a person with a serious mental illness start working closely with you on a job? (% willing)	28.6%	22.0%	35.2%
Would you be willing or unwilling to have a person with serious mental illness as a neighbor? (% willing)	33.1%	26.3%	39.9%
Perceived discrimination and belief in recovery			
Do you agree or disagree that discrimination against people with mental illness is a serious problem? (% agree)	58.2%	49.9%	66.4%
Do you agree or disagree that most people with serious mental illness can, with treatment, get well and return to productive lives? (% agree)	55.9%	48.9%	63.2%

Source: Colleen L. Barry et al., "After Newtown: Public Opinion on Gun Policy and Mental Illness," *New England Journal of Medicine*, vol. 368, no. 12, March 21, 2013. www.nejm.org.

Adam Lanza, who murdered twenty-six people at Sandy Hook Elementary School in Newtown, Connecticut, in 2012.

Violence and Schizophrenia

The connection between violence and schizophrenia is controversial. Many medical experts and advocacy organizations state that schizophrenics are rarely violent. For example, the NIMH book *Schizophrenia* states, "People with schizophrenia are not especially prone to violence and often prefer to be left alone. Studies show that if people have no record of criminal violence before they develop schizophrenia and are not substance abusers, they are unlikely to commit crimes after they become ill."[36]

Statistics, however, offer a different perspective. Researchers at Simon Fraser University in Canada found that psychotic individuals are forty-nine to sixty-eight times more likely to commit violent acts against others than the rest of the population. A 2014 study in Sweden also found that 10.7 percent of male and 2.7 percent of female schizophrenics were convicted of a violent crime within five years of their diagnosis. The Swedish researchers concluded that schizophrenia is "associated with substantially increased rates of violent crime."[37] In line with such studies, recent surveys indicate that nearly 50 percent of Americans believe schizophrenics are far more dangerous than other people, and this contributes to the stigmatization of those with the disease.

Research also shows that schizophrenics' lives are significantly impacted by violence because they are at a higher risk of being crime victims. One study at the University of Maryland School of Medicine found that schizophrenics are fourteen times more likely to be crime victims than they are to be arrested for committing a crime. Those who are homeless and those who buy and use illegal drugs are especially vulnerable to being robbed, raped, or murdered. Many who live in group homes or halfway houses and receive Social Security checks also have their checks stolen and are subject to other abuses and crimes. This is often because most are too confused and disorganized to protect themselves and their property. This confusion also leads schizophrenics to rarely report crimes against themselves.

Special Challenges for Women

Women with schizophrenia face special challenges related to pregnancy and child rearing. Such women are unlikely to seek prenatal care, so they have more birth complications and abnormal babies than other women. Medications used to treat schizophrenia can hurt a fetus or nursing baby, so some pregnant women stop taking these medications, which worsens their psychotic symptoms. According to numerous studies, hallucinations and delusions often lead mothers to neglect or abuse their children. Because of such abuse and neglect, social services departments often place schizophrenics' babies and children in foster homes. In cases of divorce, schizophrenics are rarely awarded custody, and a 2012 study found that about half of all mothers with schizophrenia eventually lose custody of their children.

Some experts believe that with proper education and assistance, schizophrenics can be good parents. However, children who grow up with a schizophrenic mother are at increased risk for psychological and social problems and even death because of exposure to odd and dangerous situations. One mother starved her daughter because voices said the girl was evil. Another stabbed her child for the same reason. One adult child wrote that when she was young, her mother ran naked through the house, screaming at the child's friend that the friend's parents were plotting against them. After that, she never brought friends home. "I feel like I lost my whole childhood," said another adult. "I lost my family, I lost birthdays and holidays, trips to the beach and all the family stuff people take for granted."

Quoted in Jeanne M. Kaiser, "Victimized Twice: The Reasonable Efforts Requirement in Child Protection Cases When Parents Have a Mental Illness," *Whittier Journal of Child and Family Advocacy*, vol. 11, no. 1, 2011, p. 12.

Another reason many such crimes go unreported is that police often dismiss complaints by psychotic people as delusional. Advocates are currently trying to educate schizophrenics about the need to report such crimes and are training them in ways to do so. Education programs for law enforcement personnel that stress the need to treat mentally ill people respectfully and calmly are also under way.

Consequences of Stigma

Even though schizophrenics are at increased risk for committing and being victims of violence, many who are not violent find the resulting stigma to be unfair and devastating. Psychiatrists at Leipzig University in Germany note, "Stigmatization is a dimension of suffering added to the illness experience, and has been found to lead to social isolation, limited life chances and delayed help-seeking behavior."[38] Stigma also damages self-esteem. Indeed, one schizophrenic who calls herself "N" writes that after her diagnosis, being rejected by others at her graduate school led to a sense of worthlessness that worsened her symptoms so much that "I descended into a state of stunning dysfunction."[39]

Many schizophrenics experience similar rejection by family, friends, and coworkers. A patient named Audrey remembers, "The hardest thing I experienced in high school was that because my friends could not handle my being sick, they abandoned me. Now I was completely alone and felt extremely alienated."[40] Although some families and friends continue to love and support those with schizophrenia, studies indicate that about 75 percent of schizophrenics experience some degree of social isolation.

> "Stigmatization is a dimension of suffering added to the illness experience, and has been found to lead to social isolation, limited life chances and delayed help-seeking behavior."[38]
>
> —Psychiatrists Beate Schulze and Matthias C. Angermeyer of Leipzig University.

Stigma also motivates many schizophrenics to advise others with the disease not to tell people outside their families about it. A patient named Jeff states, "You shouldn't tell the people you work with. They label you as a nut job."[41] Indeed, many employers admit that they will not hire people with severe mental illnesses because they are afraid of such individuals, even though this is illegal under the Americans with Disabilities Act, which prohibits discrimination against people with mental or physical disabilities. Many schizophrenics thus conceal their disease when applying for a job (which is legal to do except when applying for certain types of jobs, such as those in law enforcement). However, even when hired, many schizophrenics' odd, irresponsible, or dangerous behaviors get them fired. According to the NAMI, fewer than 15 percent of schizo-phrenics are employed.

Advocates and patients attempt to diminish stigma and discrimi-nation by educating the public about the disorder. Some programs, such as the Compeer Program, sponsor activities that bring mentally ill and healthy people together so they will view each other as indi-viduals. Some programs use humor to achieve this goal. The Stand Up for Mental Health program, for example, teaches people with severe mental illnesses to combat stigma with stand-up comedy. These types of programs also help diminish the isolation many schizophrenics ex-perience. One schizophrenic named Carol states that Compeer "has helped me to stay out of the hospital and . . . to maintain my stability. . . . I no longer want to curl up and cry."[42]

Life Expectancy

However, many factors besides stigma prevent schizophrenics from leading complete and healthy lives. In fact, their life expectancy is about twenty years less than the general public. Those who are home-less are at particular risk of dying from either a criminal act or from developing a lethal infection due to illegal drug use, promiscuous be-havior, or poor sanitation. Another reason for the diminished life ex-pectancy among schizophrenics is that they commit suicide at a rate ten to thirteen times higher than that of other people. About half of all schizophrenics attempt suicide at some point. Sometimes this results from delusions about being able to fly, which lead the individual to do things like jump off buildings. Other times it results from despair.

The shorter life expectancy also stems from loss of the ability to feel pain and to describe physical symptoms to a doctor. When schizophrenics do receive medical care, most do not follow doctors' instructions, either. Many die from heart disease or cancer, since 80 to 90 percent are heavy smokers; many also abuse alcohol and drugs and do not follow a healthy diet or exercise plan.

Others die from fires they start while smoking. Often their mental confusion prevents them from understanding the need to extinguish lit cigarettes. Some start fires deliberately in response to hallucinations or delusions. In one 2014 case, fifty-eight-year-old Patricia Bryan died at a care facility in England after deliberately setting a carpet on fire. An investigation revealed that Bryan had set numerous previous fires and was not allowed to have her own cigarette lighter. However, she kept buying lighters when she shopped in the community. She was allowed to shop independently because British laws, like those in the United States, mandate that the mentally ill be allowed to live in the least restrictive environment possible.

Mental health advocates are trying to close the life expectancy gap by encouraging doctors to promote regular exercise and healthy eating among their patients. Several studies show that schizophrenics who do aerobic exercise and strength training often experience improved mental and physical health. However, most schizophrenics do not adhere to exercise, diet, or nonsmoking plans, and a 2013 study in the *British Journal of Psychiatry* reported that "this mortality gap is widening."[43]

"The hardest thing I experienced in high school was that because my friends could not handle my being sick, they abandoned me."[40]

—Schizophrenia patient Audrey.

Living a Satisfying, Independent Life

Schizophrenics who have the best chance of improving their physical and mental health are aware they are sick and undergo successful ongoing treatment. Those with anosognosia and those for whom treatment is ineffective have minimal chances of ever living independently or holding a job. Many such patients live with family or in supported-living or inpatient facilities.

On the other hand, although few schizophrenics live what can be considered a "normal" life, some overcome their challenges and function productively, even maintaining prestigious careers. For example, psychologist Frederick Frese, who has had schizophrenia since age twenty-five, has counseled and advocated for mentally ill people for more than forty years. He teaches at two medical schools in Ohio, is married, and has four grown children. Elyn Saks, a law professor at the University of Southern California, is another schizophrenic who excels in her field. Saks believes that although she constantly struggles with psychotic symptoms, her work helps keep her stable. As she put it in a *Scientific American* article, "Work focuses my mind and provides a sense of self-esteem."[44]

Caring for a person with schizophrenia can be very challenging for family members, many of whom experience emotions such as anger, helplessness, frustration, fear, and shame. Getting support and setting realistic goals can help.

Some schizophrenics who forge productive lives learn to embrace what schizophrenia does for them. John Cadigan, an artist, has said that his disease profoundly influences his artwork. "When you have a brain disorder it unlocks parts of the brain I think normal people don't have any knowledge of. I think I translate that into my woodcuts."[45]

Family Challenges

As hard as life is for people with schizophrenia, in some respects it is even more difficult for their families. Parents and siblings face a unique variety of circumstances that lead to ongoing emotional, economic, safety, and social concerns. For example, as her son's behaviors and mental state deteriorated over several years, Randye Kaye says that she felt increasingly "angry, helpless, frustrated, and terrified. And ashamed."[46]

Many family members also comment that caring for a schizophrenic is more challenging than caring for someone with a physical disease such as cancer. Although caring for any sick person is stressful and demanding, many caregivers find that others offer compassion and are willing to help care for people with physical disorders. However, most are fearful and avoid families who have a member with a mental disorder. As one mother of a schizophrenic man states, "Some friends quit talking to us."[47] Many families therefore avoid telling others about the diagnosis. In fact, one study found that one-third of the wives married to a schizophrenic stop interacting with friends or even move to a new area to avoid acquaintances. Many people with a schizophrenic family member also stop going places with the schizophrenic because they know he or she is likely to act strangely and disruptively in restaurants, parks, or friends' homes.

Many family members also experience caregiver burnout, mental and physical health problems, and economic hardships because they have no time to attend to their own needs and may have to stop working to care for the schizophrenic. This can lead them to resent, reject, ridicule, and lash out at the schizophrenic, which experts say often exacerbates psychotic symptoms and contributes to self-destructive behaviors. The American Psychiatric Association stresses the importance of caregivers treating schizophrenics with respect. "People with mental illness need to know that they will continue to be seen as people—your brother, best friend, daughter . . . [not referred to with labels like] 'crazy,' 'nuts,' 'psych,' 'schizo,' 'retard' and 'lunatic' that may seem insignificant, but really aren't."[48] Studies show that schizophrenics whose families are supportive, accept the reality of the disease, and actively help them set realistic goals have the best chances of leading productive lives.

Experts say it is easier for families to be supportive and accepting when they make time to care for themselves and when they set limits on which behaviors will not be tolerated. For example, families are at high risk of being attacked by violent schizophrenics. In most cases schizophrenics who commit violent acts do so to protect themselves from paranoid delusions, and family members are often the ones whom schizophrenics believe are plotting against them. Experts thus advise

John Hinckley Jr. and Insanity Defense Laws

On March 30, 1981, John Hinckley Jr. tried to assassinate President Ronald Reagan. He claimed he was trying to impress actress Jodie Foster, whom his schizophrenic delusions led him to stalk. Hinckley's acts highlight the degree to which such delusions can influence behavior and also illustrate some of the controversies surrounding the legal aspects of mental illness. A court found Hinckley not guilty by reason of insanity. He was sentenced to confinement at St. Elizabeth's Hospital in Washington, DC. The verdict enraged the public, and Congress even rewrote some of the insanity laws to prevent the mentally ill from not being punished for heinous crimes. Some states even outlawed the insanity defense.

While at St. Elizabeth's, Hinckley exchanged letters with serial killer Ted Bundy and continued to collect information on Foster. Yet when he applied for privileges to visit his family, he was granted them on several occasions, even though prosecutors presented evidence that he was still dangerous. There was further outrage in 2013, when a federal judge granted Hinckley the freedom to live outside a mental hospital because several psychiatrists testified that he was no longer dangerous. However, the judge did not grant Hinckley unlimited freedom, because he and prosecutors noted that Hinckley "continues to exhibit deceptive behavior even when there are no symptoms of psychosis or depression." In other words, Hinckley was known to con his doctors into thinking he was cured of his schizophrenia when he was still sick and dangerous.

Quoted in Matt Zapotosky and Ann E. Marimow, "Federal Judge Grants More Freedom to John Hinckley Jr., Reagan's Would-Be Assassin," *Washington Post*, December 20, 2013. www.washingtonpost.com.

families to let the schizophrenic know that they will report and prosecute any violent behavior and will ban the schizophrenic from the home. However, when the schizophrenic is a child, this may not be possible. The Schofields, whose daughter, Jani, was diagnosed at age five, had to rent two apartments—one for Jani and one parent, the other for the other parent and their baby son—to prevent Jani from attacking the baby when she came home from her many hospitalizations.

In other cases if a schizophrenic has not yet committed a crime, authorities will not arrest or forcibly put him or her in a hospital. Thus, parents like Pat Spoerl, whose adult son, John, constantly threatened her, are forced to live in terror. Spoerl carefully locked her bedroom door to protect herself, until she could no longer tolerate the stress. She moved away and refused to tell John where she was.

Challenges for Siblings

Siblings of schizophrenics also face unique challenges related to being frightened, embarrassed, and resentful of the schizophrenic. Many do not bring friends over and stay away from home as much as possible. In fact, a woman named Sandy revealed on the World Fellowship for Schizophrenia and Allied Disorders website that her childhood home was such an unpleasant place because of her schizophrenic sister that she never brought friends there; when she became engaged, her parents had never met her fiancé.

The British journalist Clea Simon, who grew up with two older schizophrenic siblings, feared that she too would someday become

Siblings of a person with schizophrenia face unique challenges. Some refuse to bring friends home, or they try to stay away from their own homes as much as possible.

ill. "When you see your brother or sister grow up and change from your brother and sister to something scary and weird and alien, you just think that's what happens," she says. "You think that when you hit 16, you're allowed to date, and drive, and then you're hospitalized."[49] Simon also developed post-traumatic stress disorder and experienced terrifying flashbacks to situations in which her brother or sister terrorized her.

Although many siblings resent their schizophrenic family members, some find that living with a mentally ill person teaches valuable life lessons. Randye Kaye's daughter, Ali, for example, was saddened by what her brother's illness did to their family, but she wrote on her college application, "My brother has taught me a lot; I've learned that even when I have small failures, I can still move on. Knowing that it's hard for him to function on a daily basis makes me appreciate all I have."[50]

Support Resources

Many family members say the best way to cope with these challenges is to participate in support groups and other educational and support programs such as the NAMI's Family-to-Family program, which is taught by trained family members of mentally ill people. Talking with others going through similar challenges can be extremely helpful and can teach people strategies that work for others. Most importantly, affected people say such support makes them feel less alone. One woman commented that she found it comforting to discover that most of the parents of schizophrenics in her support group also felt guilty about their genes causing the disease.

Programs like Family-to-Family also train families to help schizophrenics get back on their feet after hospitalizations and to respond appropriately to delusions and hallucinations. For example, experts recommend not becoming angry or argumentative about such symptoms, but at the same time letting the schizophrenic know that his or her perceptions are inaccurate and false. According to the NAMI, studies indicate that families who participated in Family-to-Family "demonstrated greater feelings of empowerment and reduced displeasure and worry about the family member who lives with mental illness."[51] For families torn apart and devastated by schizophrenia, such empowerment can be a welcome relief.

CHAPTER 4

Can Schizophrenia Be Treated or Cured?

Although there is no cure for schizophrenia, many patients benefit from treatment with antipsychotic drugs, along with psychotherapy and social support programs. Most schizophrenics are treated by psychiatrists, who are medical doctors and can prescribe medications; by psychologists, who administer psychotherapy; and by social workers, who help with social- and life-skills training. Before deinstitutionalization, most schizophrenics were treated in mental hospitals, but today many are treated as outpatients in psychiatrists' offices or community clinics after one or more hospitalizations. Many relapse, or experience recurring symptoms, even when on medication. They must be rehospitalized to be restabilized. As many as half of all people with schizophrenia receive no treatment at all, often because of anosognosia (being unaware of one's illness).

Phases of Treatment

Whichever therapies are involved, psychiatrists refer to three phases of treatment: the acute, stabilization, and stable phases. The goal in the acute phase is to reduce symptoms with medications. This is usually done in a psychiatric hospital, where patients can be restrained to prevent them from harming themselves or others. Psychiatrists may need to try a variety of medications to find a drug and dosages that work, and this can take days or months.

During the stabilization phase, doctors attempt to keep the patient's symptoms under control so long-term treatment can be established (the stable phase). Stabilization usually takes about six months. In the stable phase patients and their therapists work to continue to control symptoms so they can focus on improving patients' ability to function and interact with others. Most schizophrenics require ongoing lifetime treatment and monitoring.

However, even with ideal combinations of treatments, many schizophrenics do not recover from the acute phase or become stable. Overall, studies indicate that around 25 percent recover from the acute phase over a ten-year period and can live independently; 25 percent experience some improvement from appropriate medications and can live relatively independently; 25 percent improve minimally because they do not respond well to medications; 15 percent remain hospitalized with no improvement; and 10 percent die, usually from suicide.

Antipsychotic Drugs

The first course of treatment is antipsychotic drugs. Until these drugs were invented in the 1950s, no effective treatments for schizophrenia existed, and experts noted that few patients got better. Pre-1950s treatments consisted of "wrapping them in wet towels, locking them in a padded cell, frontal lobotomies [cutting out the frontal lobe of the brain] if the behavior was really out of control. So when anti-psychotic medications did evolve and they did reduce psychotic symptoms, it was like the heavens had opened,"[52] states Dr. Sophia Vinogradov of the University of California–San Francisco.

Paul Charpentier of the Rhône-Poulenc pharmaceutical company in France synthesized the first antipsychotic, chlorpromazine, on December 11, 1951, intending it to be an anesthetic for use in surgery. In 1952 the French surgeon Henri Laborit found that some doses of chlorpromazine calmed patients without making them sleep. Laborit encouraged psychiatrists to try chlorpromazine on psychotic patients, and the results were very positive. For the first time, a medication calmed patients without completely sedating them and also diminished or banished

> "When anti-psychotic medications did evolve and they did reduce psychotic symptoms, it was like the heavens had opened."[52]
>
> —Dr. Sophia Vinogradov of the University of California–San Francisco.

psychotic symptoms. Today there are many different antipsychotic drugs. Most can be administered by mouth or injection. Long-acting injectable drugs are usually given to patients with anosognosia or to those who will not take oral medications. Fast-acting injectable medications are used in emergency rooms to quickly treat agitated patients. Different drugs work best for different patients, and in some cases combinations of drugs work best. In some instances, however, these drugs are not effective at all.

Types of Antipsychotics

The main classes of antipsychotics are the first-generation, or typical, antipsychotics, and the second-generation, or atypical, drugs. Examples of typical antipsychotics include chlorpromazine, haloperidol, and perphenazine. Atypical drugs include clozapine, olanzapine, quetiapine, risperidone, and ziprasidone. Both typical and atypical antipsychotics have side effects such as weight gain, high blood sugar, tardive dyskinesia (involuntary twitches and other body motions), drowsiness, and others. Some experts believe atypical antipsychotics have fewer side effects than typical drugs, but most studies indicate that both types have many of the same side effects.

Most studies indicate that overall, clozapine is the most effective antipsychotic. However, it is rarely prescribed in the United States, because it can lead to a decrease in white blood cells. This condition, known as agranulocytosis, can be fatal. Because of this risk, patients must have frequent blood tests, which most do not wish to endure. Many doctors thus do not prescribe clozapine unless nothing else works.

Although all types of antipsychotics are often effective, psychiatrists are not sure exactly how they work. They do know that the medications change neurotransmitter activity and increase the number of neural synapses and glial cells in the brain and that different antipsychotics mainly affect different neurotransmitters. Recent research shows that antipsychotics also affect the immune system. This finding complements other research that indicates immune cells and immune chemicals may contribute to causing schizophrenia by increasing inflammation in the brain. A 2013 study, for instance, found that clozapine, haloperidol, quetiapine, and risperidone—all antipsychotics—

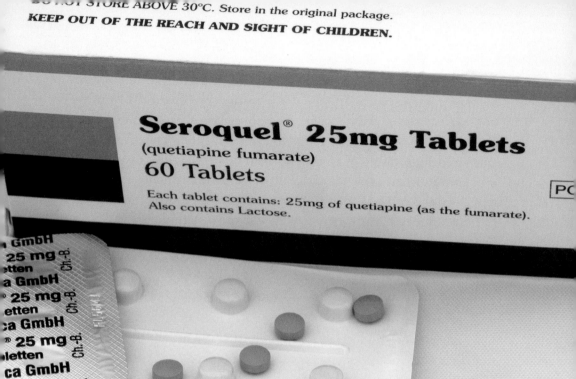

One of the antipsychotic drugs used to treat schizophrenia is quetiapine, sold under the name Seroquel. These types of drugs often have side effects such as weight gain and drowsiness.

raise blood levels of immune chemicals that decrease inflammation and lower levels of chemicals that increase inflammation. However, even with this type of knowledge, "The bottom line is that we really don't know how they [antipsychotic drugs] work," writes E. Fuller Torrey. "But then, we don't yet know how aspirin works either."[53]

Other Treatments

In addition to primary treatment with antipsychotics, psychiatrists often prescribe antianxiety drugs, antidepressants, and drugs to counteract antipsychotics' side effects. Antidepressants, in particular, can boost the effects of antipsychotics and help with mood-related symptoms.

When all types of medications are ineffective, some patients receive electroconvulsive therapy (ECT). During an ECT treatment, doctors attach electrodes to the patient's head and deliver an electric shock that causes a brief seizure. This often calms patients and reduces their symptoms. ECT has been labeled as abusive, but doctors say that modern procedures are not painful or traumatic. Most of the unfavorable views of ECT came about because early treatments from the late 1930s through the 1960s did not use general anesthesia and employed high doses of electricity. Patients frequently experienced broken bones, memory loss, and other undesirable effects, and they described the convulsion as traumatic. Today doctors use general anesthesia and well-controlled electric currents. Although ECT is effective, doctors do not yet know how it works.

Although medications are the first line of treatment for schizophrenia, experts emphasize the importance of psychosocial treatments as well. Psychosocial treatments include cognitive behavioral therapy, which involves therapists helping patients develop positive ways of thinking and behaving; family therapy, which involves patients' families in supporting them; and supported education and employment programs, in which coaches help patients go back to school or get a job and provide ongoing assistance as needed. Cognitive rehabilitation, a therapy designed especially for people with schizophrenia, is also widely employed. Cognitive rehabilitation helps patients learn to express their needs, understand others, and function socially. One of the most successful types of rehabilitation programs is the clubhouse model, in which staff members supervise groups of patients who live and work together and support each other in mastering aspects of daily living. Since many schizophrenics abuse alcohol and street drugs, in many cases drug rehabilitation therapy is part of rehabilitation programs as well.

However, psychiatrists emphasize that psychosocial treatments by themselves are ineffective. As the NIMH notes, "Psychosocial treatments can help people with schizophrenia who are already stabilized on antipsychotic medication."[54]

Predicting a Good Outcome

Research indicates that the key elements for helping patients achieve positive treatment outcomes are prompt, early treatment with drugs and ongoing help with social, psychological, and life skills. Recent research has especially focused on the importance of starting drug and psychosocial treatments immediately after symptoms emerge. To pro-

Percentages of Schizophrenics Who Recover After Ten and Thirty Years

Even with modern medical treatments, many schizophrenics do not get better. However, more and more are achieving good results. Recent studies indicate that after ten years, about 25 percent recover completely, 25 percent recover quite a bit, 25 percent improve somewhat, 15 percent remain hospitalized with no improvement, and 10 percent die, usually from suicide. Thirty years after being diagnosed, the outlook for some improves, as aging can diminish symptoms.

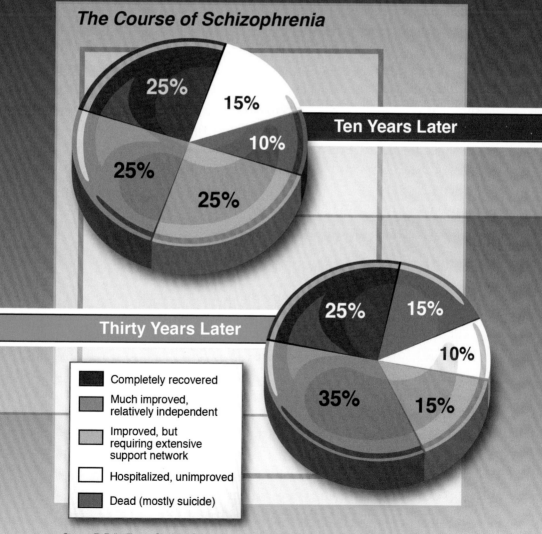

The Course of Schizophrenia

Ten Years Later

25% 15% 10% 25% 25%

Thirty Years Later

25% 15% 10% 35% 15%

Legend:
- Completely recovered
- Much improved, relatively independent
- Improved, but requiring extensive support network
- Hospitalized, unimproved
- Dead (mostly suicide)

Source: E. Fuller Torrey, *Surviving Schizophrenia*, 6th ed., New York: Harper Perennial, 2013, p. 102.

mote early treatment, the NIMH funded the RAISE (Recovery After an Initial Schizophrenia Episode) Connection program to jump-start new early intervention programs. RAISE and similar programs also emphasize the importance of letting patients share in the decision-making process regarding their treatment. "I think the most important thing about this approach is that it is oriented around the notion that people can achieve and people can adapt," says psychiatrist Lisa B. Dixon. "If you approach people with a sense of promise, hope, and shared decision-making they can . . . learn to manage their illness."[55]

One successful early intervention program in Maine, called the Portland Identification and Early Referral Program, has helped many people recover after their first psychotic episode. It has also been shown to save money because it reduces first-episode hospitalizations by more than 25 percent. Tiffany Martinez is one individual who benefited from this program; she was referred to it by counselors at her college after she began having paranoid delusions and contemplating suicide. She was given low doses of antipsychotics, along with counseling and education about schizophrenia. Therapists also arranged for her to receive special accommodations at her school. As a result, Martinez completed college and earned a master's degree in psychiatric nursing.

Other Predictive Factors

Another factor found to be a valid predictor of treatment success is whether the individual was considered to be relatively "normal" before the emergence of schizophrenia. That is, if the person made friends, did well in school, and did not get into trouble as a child, he or she has a better chance of some degree of recovery. Experts believe this may be because people who functioned well before schizophrenia struck are less likely to have negative symptoms once they become schizophrenic. Antipsychotic drugs do not diminish negative symptoms, so those with negative symptoms, especially those with anosognosia, have a poor prognosis.

Closely related to this predictive factor is the fact that those who develop schizophrenia at an older age have a greater chance of recovery. Researchers at the University of Illinois College of Medicine believe this is true because people who have had more time to learn

Alternative Treatments: Omega-3 Fatty Acids

Some patients try alternative treatments for schizophrenia, such as special diets or dietary supplements, although psychiatrists say there is no proof such treatments are effective in treating the disease. There is, however, some evidence that taking omega-3 fatty acid supplements may be helpful when used in conjunction with antipsychotics.

Studies indicate that omega-3 fatty acids may be effective because schizophrenics metabolize phospholipids and polyunsaturated fatty acids—types of fat molecules—abnormally. However, although several studies show that taking omega-3 fatty acid capsules along with antipsychotics reduces psychotic symptoms more than antipsychotics alone, other studies find no such results. The federal Agency for Healthcare Research and Quality has thus concluded that further research on this question is needed.

and develop social skills are more likely to be able to draw on these experiences during rehabilitation.

These researchers and others find that gender also helps predict treatment success. The University of Illinois team followed male and female schizophrenics of the same age for twenty years. They found that 61 percent of the females compared to 41 percent of the males experienced a period of recovery at some time. In general, the women also responded better to antipsychotic drugs. Some experts believe this may occur because the female sex hormone estrogen influences dopamine activity in the brain, which has a natural antipsychotic effect. However, the University of Illinois study found that older women who are past menopause—when estrogen levels fall dramatically— also recover better than men, so these investigators believe "if estrogen is a factor, other factors may be even more important in regard to their psychosis."[56] Further research on this topic is under way.

Another biological factor that influences prognosis is that those with no family history of schizophrenia have a much better prognosis than those with family members who have schizophrenia. Interestingly, those with a family history of bipolar disorder or depression and those with no family history of mental illness also have a better prognosis. In addition, people with no enlarged ventricles or other structural brain abnormalities have a better prognosis. Psychiatrists find that the more positive predictive factors an individual has, the better the prognosis. Thus, a female who develops schizophrenia at age forty after leading a fairly normal life is more likely to respond well to treatment than a male who becomes schizophrenic at age eighteen after years of increasingly odd behaviors.

Noncompliance with Treatment

The most common reason patients do not achieve good treatment results is that many—more than 70 percent—stop taking their medications or refuse to take them at all. Patients do this for a variety of reasons. In many cases antipsychotics have very unpleasant side effects. As one man stated, "I would rather get sick [with psychosis] than get the side effects [from medicine]."[57] Some patients stop taking their medications because they notice symptoms lessen or disappear and believe they no longer need treatment. According to the *World Journal of Biological Psychiatry*, many also do not accept the fact that "long-term treatment is necessary for all patients with schizophrenia."[58] Some patients who stop taking their medications state that doctors never explained the need for ongoing treatment.

Many schizophrenics blame their refusal to take medication or to seek any treatment on the stigma of mental illness. Many think that if they do not admit to themselves or others that they are sick, no one will notice, and therefore they will be spared the hurtful names and social isolation that often accompanies schizophrenia. Others believe that if they seek medical help, doctors will automatically label them as crazy and lock them up indefinitely. In other cases, according to National Public Radio journalist Amy Standen, patients "say they don't want to get rid of their hallucinations because they are a part of who they are."[59] One woman, for instance, stated that she would not take medicine because she believed it was unnatural to change her natural brain chemistry.

In his book *Recovered, Not Cured*, Richard McLean wrote that he started and then stopped taking antipsychotics because "life was less interesting . . . reality enveloped me in greyness and boredom. . . . It's not that I missed being psychotic; the difference was that I went from being waves on a beach to a particle of sand."[60] Studies indicate that involving patients as partners in choosing their medications, as well as educating them about the need for lifelong compliance, can motivate them to keep taking their medication. Many doctors are thus attempting to involve patients (coherent ones, at least) in these decisions.

Involuntary Medication

However, sometimes there is a need to medicate and hospitalize individuals against their will—called involuntary medication and hospitalization, a controversial practice. Most psychiatrists believe that forcibly medicating people who pose a threat to themselves or others

The Legal Basis for Involuntary Treatment and Hospitalization

There are two main legal doctrines that give courts the power to order that mentally ill people be treated or hospitalized against their will. The first is called *parens patriae*, meaning "parent of one's country." It allows the government to act as a guardian for those, such as children, who are unable to care for themselves. This power also applies when people are not aware they are ill and need help.

The second doctrine is the government's right to protect the public from dangerous individuals. Different state laws vary, but most allow doctors, family members, legal guardians, and government employees such as police officers to file a petition for emergency commitment of dangerous psychotic individuals. Some states only allow this if the individuals are an immediate threat to themselves or others. This often leads families to live in constant fear of a schizophrenic who threatens violence but does not actually have a weapon.

After a petition is filed, one or sometimes two doctors must examine the person to certify that he or she is mentally ill and should be hospitalized. In most states this emergency commitment lasts for seventy-two hours. Hospital directors or family members can then petition for the patient to be held longer. A judge then decides how long the person can be involuntarily hospitalized and treated.

is necessary to protect the public. They point to instances in which schizophrenics who were not medicated committed violent crimes.

However, others view this as an assault on schizophrenic individuals' civil rights. Indeed, organizations like the American Civil Liberties Union and the Bazelon Center for Mental Health Law say schizophrenics have the right to be insane if they so choose. The Bazelon Center also notes that "fear of being deprived of autonomy discourages people from receiving care . . . the experience of forced treatment is traumatic and humiliating, often exacerbating a person's mental health condition."[61] Torrey is one of many psychiatrists who oppose such views, writing in his book *American Psychosis*, "The freedom to be insane is a cruel hoax, perpetrated on those who cannot think clearly by those who will not think clearly."[62]

> "When someone does something without your consent, including forcibly injecting you with medication, it can feel very dehumanizing. It feels like you have no control over your own being."[63]
>
> —Schizophrenia patient Ron Schraiber.

Patients have diverse views on forced medication. Ron Schraiber, a paranoid schizophrenic, opposes this practice. As he puts it, "When someone does something without your consent, including forcibly injecting you with medication, it can feel very dehumanizing. It feels like you have no control over your own being."[63] In contrast, several studies show that 60 to 70 percent of the schizophrenics who were forcibly medicated later agree that if the situation recurred, they would want to be forcibly medicated again because they recognize they were unable to make rational decisions. For instance, a patient named Erin L. Hawkes writes, "I cried, I screamed, I was terrified and humiliated; I was protesting as fiercely as I could, but still they held me down, tied me up, and violated my body with needles. Thank you, I now say. . . . Had I not been at times treated involuntarily, I would never have become well."[64]

In the United States, state laws on involuntary commitment and medication vary. Following deinstitutionalization in the 1960s, most state laws made it almost impossible to forcibly commit patients unless they actually committed a crime. For example, in the 1990s the Gambs family of California tried for five years to force their schizophrenic son, Rodger, into treatment because he constantly threatened them. Authorities said Rodger was not dangerous enough to be medicated against his will. His parents were only able to file criminal charges and have him hospitalized for treatment after he stole two guns to protect himself against delusions that vampires were living nearby.

Similar events and tragedies, such as the case in which a schizophrenic off his medications pushed Kendra Webdale under a subway train in New York, led some states to change these laws. In 1999 New York passed Kendra's Law, which allows judges to order mentally ill people at risk for violence to accept treatment instead of being committed to a hospital. But even with such changes, involuntary medication is still difficult in some states. For instance, in 2010, after seventeen-year-old Richard Wilson of Wisconsin threatened his parents with a knife, they tried to commit him for treatment. But

A patient spends a quiet moment in his room at a psychiatric hospital. Since the deinstitutionalization movement, which began in the 1960s, forced or involuntary commitments are nearly impossible unless the person has committed a crime.

according to journalist Meg Kissinger, "One counselor after another told them the same thing: Unless he's got a gun in his hand, he won't meet the requirement."[65]

Controversies About Antipsychotics

Other controversies exist about whether antipsychotics do more harm than good. Although most psychiatrists believe antipsychotics are beneficial, some oppose their use. The British psychiatrist Joanna Moncrieff calls them "the new tranquillisers"[66] used to subdue patients. Psychiatrist Peter Breggin writes that "the drugs work by producing a chemical lobotomy . . . [keeping patients] too

Alternative Treatments: Gluten-Free Diet

There is some indication that following a gluten-free diet may prove to be an effective component of treatment for some schizophrenics. Gluten is a protein found in foods such as wheat, rye, barley, and farina. Many people who are sensitive to or cannot tolerate gluten avoid these foods and choose gluten-free ones like corn, rice, flax, or soy.

In 1961 doctors at the Institute of Pennsylvania Hospital first proposed a link between schizophrenia and gluten after noticing that several young adults with schizophrenia had celiac syndrome as babies. Celiac syndrome involves an intolerance for gluten that leads to small intestine damage and a subsequent inability to absorb nutrients. Later studies found that more than 5 percent of schizophrenics have blood levels of gluten antibodies comparable to those seen in people with celiac disease. Some experts have thus proposed that antibodies to gluten may contribute to schizophrenia and that a gluten-free diet may be an effective treatment. A 2014 study at the University of Maryland–Baltimore indicated that such a diet reduced some symptoms in two schizophrenics who had gluten antibodies and also diminished side effects from antipsychotics. However, larger studies are needed to determine if a gluten-free diet is truly effective.

apathetic to complain or even to recognize their abnormal movements."[67]

Other experts believe short-term treatment with antipsychotics is beneficial, but long-term treatment is harmful and prevents schizophrenics from functioning well. Some antipsychotics control psychotic symptoms by diminishing the amount of dopamine in the brain. Dutch psychiatrist Lex Wunderink believes that this hampers patients' ability to think clearly and function independently. In a 2013 study, Wunderink found that although schizophrenics who stop taking their medications experience more relapses of psychotic symptoms, they function better overall. He notes, "The functional domain is what matters most from a patient perspective,"[68] since many patients say they prefer to live with psychotic symptoms rather than endure the side effects of antipsychotics. Wunderink believes that giving patients who do not have debilitating psychotic symptoms lower doses of antipsychotics may also help them function better.

> "I cried, I screamed, I was terrified and humiliated; I was protesting as fiercely as I could, but still they held me down, tied me up, and violated my body with needles. Thank you, I now say."[64]
>
> —Schizophrenia patient Erin L. Hawkes.

Some recent studies also show that high doses of antipsychotics reduce brain size, but researchers are not yet sure about the significance of these findings. Many psychiatrists assert that such brain abnormalities were documented in schizophrenics long before antipsychotics were invented, so the medications should not be blamed.

However, given the fact that many patients do not wish to take antipsychotics, some psychiatrists are developing cognitive training methods to help schizophrenics deal with symptoms. Sophia Vinogradov and her associates are using computerized training programs to teach schizophrenics to tune out hallucinations and distracting thoughts and to distinguish reality from fantasy. In a 2012 study, these researchers found that an eighty-hour program improved patients' ability to distinguish sensations and perceptions generated in their brains from those generated externally.

Furthermore, fMRI scans showed that before the training, the schizophrenics' brains had no activity in the medial prefrontal cortex when they were asked to distinguish reality from fantasy. After the training, their brains showed some activity in this area, though the amount was abnormally low. The researchers believe further studies are needed before such programs can be implemented, because "we do not know which aspects of the cognitive training were most responsible for the behavioral and neural improvements."[69]

Outlook for the Future

Given the recent advances in cognitive and biological research, scientists are hopeful that schizophrenia treatment can be improved in the future. A 2014 study in which researchers identified 108 genes that contribute to schizophrenia is one advance that has instilled newfound optimism about the possibility of formulating new drugs based on these genetic targets. As senior study author Michael O'Donovan said, "The wealth of new findings have the potential to kick-start the development of new treatments in schizophrenia, a process which has been stalled for the last 60 years."[70]

With this new knowledge, for the first time scientists are also studying ways to prevent schizophrenia by analyzing genomes and developing various interventions such as stress reduction, abstinence from street drugs, or low-dose antipsychotic drug treatments for those deemed at high risk for schizophrenia. Other research is exploring whether schizophrenia can be prevented using prenatal and postnatal dietary supplements. For example, a 2013 study at the University of Colorado–Denver found that giving choline (a B vitamin) supplements to pregnant women and newborns can reduce the brain damage that leads to schizophrenia. Overall, states the NIMH, "This is a time of hope for people with schizophrenia and their families."[71]

"This is a time of hope for people with schizophrenia and their families."[71]

—The NIMH.

SOURCE NOTES

Introduction: Schizophrenia: A Personal and Societal Burden

1. Richard Mead, *Medical Precepts and Cautions*, trans. Thomas Stack. London: Brindley, 1751, p. 74.

2. Mark Olfson, "Cost and Clinical Implications of Treating Schizophrenia," Psychiatrist.com. www.psychiatrist.com.

3. Richard R. Friedman, "A Solution That Now Looks Crazy," *New York Times*, January 13, 2014. www.nytimes.com.

4. Gordon C. Shen and Lonnie R. Snowden, "Institutionalization of Deinstitutionalization: A Cross-National Analysis of Mental Health System Reform," *International Journal of Mental Health Systems*, vol. 8, 2014. www.ijmhs.com.

Chapter 1: What Is Schizophrenia?

5. National Alliance on Mental Illness, "Schizophrenia," 2011. www.nami.org.

6. *Scientific American*, "Schizophrenia's Slow Evolution." www.scientificamerican.com.

7. Alan A. Baumeister et al., "Prevalence and Incidence of Severe Mental Illness in the United States: An Historical Overview," *Harvard Review of Psychiatry*, vol. 20, no.5, September/October 2012, p. 247.

8. John Haslam, *Illustrations of Madness*. Hove, UK: Routledge, 2014, pp. xxxii–xxxiii.

9. Eugen Bleuler, *Dementia Praecox or the Group of Schizophrenias*, trans. and ed. J. Zinkin. New York: International Universities, 1950, p. 59.

10. *The Merck Manual*, "Schizophrenia," 2015. www.merckmanuals.com.

11. *The Merck Manual*, "Schizophrenia."

12. Emil Kraepelin, *Dementia Praecox and Paraphrenia*, ed. George M. Robertson, trans. Mary Barclay. Edinburgh: Livingstone, 1919, pp. 236–37.

13. Quoted in Tara Parker-Pope, "The Voices of Schizophrenia," *Well* (blog), *New York Times*, September 15, 2010. http://well.blogs .nytimes.com.

14. Linda, "The First Signs of Schizophrenia," Schizophrenia.com. www.schizophrenia.com.

15. Barnaby Nelson et al., "Basic Self-Disturbance Predicts Psychosis Onset in the Ultra High Risk For Psychosis 'Prodromal' Population," *Schizophrenia Bulletin*, February 20, 2012. http://schizo phreniabulletin.oxfordjournals.org.

16. Richard McLean, *Recovered, Not Cured*. Crows Nest, Australia: Allen and Unwin, 2005, p. 76.

17. Brendan McLean, "The Difficulty in Seeing Your Own Illness," National Alliance on Mental Illness, 2011. www.nami.org.

18. Quoted in Louis A. Sass and Josef Parnas, "Schizophrenia, Consciousness, and the Self," *Schizophrenia Bulletin*, vol. 29, no. 3, 2003, p. 427.

19. Leslie N. Louis, "Schizophrenia: Senses, Sensations, and Sense," *Orthomolecular Psychiatry*, vol. 3, no. 3, 1974, p. 198.

20. Louis, "Schizophrenia," p. 197.

21. Julie Loebach Wetherell and Dilip V. Jeste, "Older Adults with Schizophrenia," *ElderCare*, vol. 3, no. 2, June 2003, p. 9.

Chapter 2: What Causes Schizophrenia?

22. Quoted in Richard Noll, *The Encyclopedia of Schizophrenia and Other Psychotic Disorders*, 3rd ed. New York: Facts On File, 2007, p. 45.

23. E. Fuller Torrey, *Surviving Schizophrenia*, 6th ed. New York: Harper Perennial, 2013, p. xv.

24. Rachel Miller and Susan E. Mason, *Diagnosis: Schizophrenia*, 2nd ed. New York: Columbia University Press, 2011, p. 37.

25. Erin A. Hazlett et al., "A Review of Structural MRI and Diffusion Tensor Imaging in Schizotypal Personality Disorder," *Current Psychiatry Reports*, vol. 14, no. 1, February 2012, p. 76.

26. Juha Veijola et al., "Longitudinal Changes in Total Brain Volume in Schizophrenia: Relation to Symptom Severity, Cognition and Antipsychotic Medication," *PLOS ONE*, vol. 9, no. 7, July 18, 2014, p. e101689.

27. National Institute of Mental Health, "Schizophrenia." www.nimh.nih.gov.

28. Torrey, *Surviving Schizophrenia*, p. 77.

29. M. Leboyer et al., "Human Endogenous Retrovirus Type W (HERV-W) in Schizophrenia: A New Avenue of Research at the Gene-Environment Interface," *World Journal of Biological Psychiatry*, vol. 14, no. 2, March 2013, p. 80.

30. Christian Caldji et al., "Maternal Care During Infancy Regulates the Development of Neural Systems Mediating the Expression of Fearfulness in the Rat," *Proceedings of the National Academy of Sciences*, vol. 95, no. 9, April 28, 1998, p. 5,335.

31. Eugene Ruby et al., "Pathways Associating Childhood Trauma to the Neurobiology of Schizophrenia," *Frontiers in Psychological and Behavioral Science*, vol. 3, no. 1, 2014, p. 1.

Chapter 3: What Is It like to Live with Schizophrenia?

32. *The Merck Manual*, "Schizophrenia."

33. Quoted in Torrey, *Surviving Schizophrenia*, p. 7.

34. Quoted in Marguerite Sechehaye, *Autobiography of a Schizophrenic Girl*. New York: Grune and Stratton, 1951, p. 22.

35. Klara Latalova, Dana Kamaradova, and Jan Prasko, "Violent Victimization of Adult Patients with Severe Mental Illness: A

Systematic Review," *Neuropsychiatric Disease and Treatment*, vol. 10, 2014, p. 1925.

36. National Institute of Mental Health, *Schizophrenia*. Middletown, DE: US Department of Health and Human Services, 2012, p. 9.

37. S. Fasel et al., "Violent Crime, Suicide, and Premature Mortality in Patients with Schizophrenia and Related Disorders: A 38-Year Total Population Study in Sweden," *Lancet Psychiatry*, vol. 1, no. 1, June 2014, p. 44.

38. Beate Schulze and Matthias C. Angermeyer, "Subjective Experiences of Stigma. A Focus Group Study of Schizophrenic Patients, Their Relatives and Mental Health Professionals," *Social Science & Medicine*, vol. 56, 2003, p. 299.

39. Quoted in David Dobbs, "Batman Returns: How Culture Shapes Muddle into Madness," *Wired*, July 27, 2012. www.wired.com.

40. Quoted in Miller and Mason, *Diagnosis*, p. 70.

41. Quoted in Miller and Mason, *Diagnosis*, p. 73.

42. Quoted in Compeer, "Success Stories," 2011. http://compeer.org.

43. Lily McNamee et al., "Schizophrenia, Poor Physical Health and Physical Activity: Evidence-Based Interventions Are Required to Reduce Major Health Inequalities," *British Journal of Psychiatry*, vol. 203, 2013, p. 239.

44. Quoted in *Scientific American*, "Diary of a High-Functioning Person with Schizophrenia," December 29, 2009. www.scientific american.com.

45. Quoted in Parker-Pope, "The Voices of Schizophrenia."

46. Randye Kaye, *Ben Behind His Voices*. Plymouth, UK: Rowman & Littlefield, 2011, p. 72.

47. Quoted in Richard Warner, *Recovery from Schizophrenia: Psychiatry and Political Economy*. London: Routledge, 2013, p. 202.

48. Jenna Bowen, "The Power of Words: Addressing the Stigma of Mental Illness," *Healthy Minds Healthy Lives* (blog), Ameri-

can Psychiatric Association, January 2, 2015. http://apahealthy minds.blogspot.com.

49. Quoted in Karen Brown, "A Burden to Be Well," American RadioWorks, 2015. http://americanradioworks.publicradio.org.

50. Quoted in Kaye, *Ben Behind His Voices*, p. 216.

51. National Alliance on Mental Illness, "Schizophrenia: Latest Research," 2015. www.nami.org.

Chapter 4: Can Schizophrenia Be Treated or Cured?

52. Quoted in Amy Standen, "Brain Training May Help Calm the Storms of Schizophrenia," *Shots* (blog), National Public Radio, November 3, 2014. www.npr.org.

53. Torrey, *Surviving Schizophrenia*, p. 182.

54. National Institute of Mental Health, "Schizophrenia: What Is Schizophrenia?" www.nimh.nih.gov.

55. Quoted in New York–Presbyterian Hospital, "Changing the Course of Schizophrenia Through Early Detection and Intervention," October/November 2013. http://nyp.org.

56. L.S. Grossman et al., "Sex Differences in Schizophrenia and Other Psychotic Disorders: A 20-Year Longitudinal Study of Psychosis and Recovery," *Comprehensive Psychiatry*, vol. 49, no. 6, 2008, p. 529.

57. Quoted in Miller and Mason, *Diagnosis*, p. 86.

58. Alkomiet Hasan et al., "World Federation of Societies of Biological Psychiatry (WFSBP) Guidelines for Biological Treatment of Schizophrenia, Part 2: Update 2012 on the Long-Term Treatment of Schizophrenia and Management of Antipsychotic-Induced Side Effects," *World Journal of Biological Psychiatry*, vol. 14, 2013, p. 4.

59. Standen, "Brain Training May Help Calm the Storms of Schizophrenia."

60. McLean, *Recovered, Not Cured*, pp. 160–61.

61. Bazelon Center for Mental Health Law, "Forced Treatment," 2014. www.bazelon.org.

62. E. Fuller Torrey, *American Psychosis*. New York: Oxford University Press, 2014, p. 148.

63. Quoted in Jens Erik Gould, "Should Involuntary Treatment for the Mentally Ill Be the Law?," *Time*, October 27, 2011. http://content.time.com.

64. Erin L. Hawkes, "Thank You for Medicating Me," *Tyee*, July 16, 2012. http://thetyee.ca.

65. Meg Kissinger, "Law Creates Barriers to Getting Care for Mentally Ill," *Milwaukee (WI) Journal Sentinel*, December 10, 2011. www.jsonline.com.

66. Joanna Moncrieff, *The Bitterest Pills*. Hampshire, UK: Palgrave MacMillan, 2013, p. 126.

67. Peter Breggin, "Antipsychotic Drugs, Their Harmful Effects, and the Limits of Tort Reform," *Huffington Post*, November 17, 2011. www.huffingtonpost.com.

68. Quoted in Nancy A. Melville, "Antipsychotics in First-Episode Psychosis: Less Is More," *Medscape Medical News*, July 16, 2013. www.medscape.com.

69. Karuna Subramaniam et al., "Computerized Cognitive Training Restores Neural Activity Within the Reality Monitoring Network in Schizophrenia," *Neuron*, vol. 73, February 23, 2012, p. 849.

70. Quoted in Matthew Dennis, "Study Identifies Genetic Locations Linked to Schizophrenia, Offering Future Treatment Hope," FirstWord Pharma, July 20, 2014. www.firstwordpharma.com.

71. National Institute of Mental Health, *Schizophrenia*, p. 2.

ORGANIZATIONS TO CONTACT

American Psychiatric Association

1000 Wilson Blvd., Suite 1825
Arlington, VA 22209
phone: (703) 907-7300
website: www.psychiatry.org

The American Psychiatric Association is a professional organization for psychiatrists that also provides information about all aspects of mental illnesses such as schizophrenia, including symptoms, causes, diagnosis, treatment, living with the disease, and research.

American Psychological Association

750 First St. NE
Washington, DC 20002
phone: (202) 336-5500
website: http://apa.org

The American Psychological Association is a professional organization for psychologists. It also offers information about all aspects of schizophrenia and other mental illnesses.

Bazelon Center for Mental Health Law

1101 Fifteenth St. NW, Suite 1212
Washington, DC 20005
phone: (202) 467-5730
website: www.bazelon.org

The Bazelon Center advocates for the rights of mentally ill people to make their own choices and to participate fully in their communities. The center promotes laws that enforce these rights and assists mentally ill people with legal matters. The website contains numerous articles about these issues.

Brain & Behavior Research Foundation

90 Park Ave., 16th Floor
New York, NY 10016
phone: (646) 681-4888
website: https://bbrfoundation.org

The Brain & Behavior Research Foundation awards mental health research grants to scientists working on methods of improving life for those with mental illnesses. The organization also provides information and support to people who wish to learn about mental illnesses, including schizophrenia.

National Alliance on Mental Illness (NAMI)

3803 N. Fairfax Dr., Suite 100
Arlington, VA 22203
phone: (703) 524-7600
website: www.nami.org

The NAMI is a national organization with chapters in all fifty states. It seeks to better the lives of mentally ill people and their families by offering information, education programs, support, and advocacy, and by sponsoring research on all aspects of mental illness. It also helps shape national policies on mental illness. Its website offers comprehensive information on all aspects of schizophrenia.

National Institute of Mental Health (NIMH)

Science Writing, Press, and Dissemination Branch
6001 Executive Blvd., Room 6200, MSC9663
Bethesda, MD 20892
phone: (866) 615-6464
website: www.nimh.nih.gov

The NIMH is a branch of the National Institutes of Health. It sponsors research on mental illnesses and provides the public with information about mental health and mental illness. Its website contains information on all aspects of schizophrenia, including causes, diagnosis, symptoms, treatment, research, and living with the disease.

Schizophrenia and Related Disorders Alliance of America (SARDAA)

PO Box 941222
Houston, TX 77094
phone: (240) 423-9432
website: www.sardaa.org

SARDAA is an education and support organization that seeks to help people with schizophrenia and their families improve their lives. It also works to diminish the stigma associated with mental illness. In addition SARDAA supports and trains Schizophrenics Anonymous groups.

Treatment Advocacy Center

200 N. Glebe Rd., Suite 801
Arlington, VA 22203
phone: (703) 294-6001
website: www.treatmentadvocacycenter.org

The Treatment Advocacy Center is a nonprofit organization that promotes laws and policies that help people with severe mental illnesses obtain appropriate treatment. It also supports research and educates the public and lawmakers about these illnesses and about the consequences of not treating individuals who pose a threat to themselves or others. Its website contains many articles about schizophrenia.

World Fellowship for Schizophrenia and Allied Disorders (WFSAD)

19 MacPherson Ave.
Toronto, Ontario, M5R 1W7, Canada
website: www.world-schizophrenia.org

The WFSAD is a global grassroots organization that strives to ease the burden of schizophrenia on patients and families through education and efforts to diminish stigma. The group conducts workshops and runs self-help groups. The WFSAD website contains educational materials and personal stories of people affected by schizophrenia.

World Health Organization (WHO)

Ave. Appia 20
1211 Geneva 27
Switzerland
phone: +41 22 791 21 11
website: www.who.int

WHO coordinates worldwide health care for the United Nations and provides leadership on global health concerns. Its website offers information about all aspects of schizophrenia and its global impact.

FOR FURTHER RESEARCH

Books

Lucy Adamson, *The Voice Within—My Life with Schizophrenia*. Surrey, UK: Grosvenor House, 2013.

Shirley Brinkerhoff, *Schizophrenia*. Broomal, PA: Mason Crest, 2013.

Aimee Houser, *Tragedy in Tucson*. Minneapolis, MN: ABDO, 2012.

Carrie Iorizzo, *Schizophrenia and Other Psychotic Disorders*. New York: Crabtree, 2014.

Carla Mooney, *Mental Illness Research*. San Diego, CA: ReferencePoint, 2012.

Peggy J. Parks, *Schizophrenia*. San Diego, CA: ReferencePoint, 2010.

Internet Sources

Neel Burton, "A Brief History of Schizophrenia," *Hide and Seek* (blog), *Psychology Today*, September 8, 2012. www.psychologytoday.com/blog/hide-and-seek/201209/brief-history-schizophrenia.

Scott O. Lilienfeld and Hal Arkowitz, "Living with Schizophrenia," *Scientific American*, February 11, 2010. www.scientificamerican.com/article/living-with-schizophrenia.

Kathleen McAuliffe, "How Your Cat Is Making You Crazy," *Atlantic*, March 2012. www.theatlantic.com/magazine/archive/2012/03/how-your-cat-is-making-you-crazy/308873.

National Alliance on Mental Illness, "Schizophrenia," 2015. www2.nami.org/Template.cfm?Section=Schizophrenia9&Template=/ContentManagement/ContentDisplay.cfm&ContentID=117961.

National Institute of Mental Health, "Schizophrenia." www.nimh.nih.gov/health/publications/schizophrenia/index.shtml.

National Institute of Mental Health, "Schizophrenia (Easy-to-Read)." www.nimh.nih.gov/health/publications/schizophrenia-easy-to-read/index.shtml.

Liz Szabo, "Early Intervention Could Change Nature of Schizophrenia," *USA Today*, December 31, 2014. www.usatoday.com/longform/news/nation/2014/12/31/early-intervention-mental-illness/18183737.

Websites

Schizophrenia and Psychosis, Psych Central (http://psychcentral.com/disorders/schizophrenia). The Psych Central website's page on schizophrenia and psychosis provides information on symptoms, types of schizophrenia, associated problems, causes, treatment, and living with the disease.

Schizophrenia, Mayo Clinic (www.mayoclinic.org/diseases-conditions/schizophrenia/basics/definition/CON-20021077?p=1). The Mayo Clinic website's page on schizophrenia offers a detailed overview of all aspects of schizophrenia, including symptoms, diagnosis, causes, treatment, and living with the disease.

Schizophrenia, Medical News Today (www.medicalnewstoday.com/sections/schizophrenia). The Medical News Today's schizophrenia section provides the latest news on schizophrenia, gathered from scientific journals.

Schizophrenia Research Forum (www.schizophreniaforum.org). The Schizophrenia Research Forum website has information on current schizophrenia research and new developments in schizophrenia care.

Understanding Schizophrenia, Helpguide (www.helpguide.org/articles/schizophrenia/schizophrenia-signs-types-and-causes.htm). The Helpguide website provides extensive information about the symptoms, causes, treatments, and effects of schizophrenia.

INDEX

PICTURE CREDITS

Cover: Mikhail Grachikov/Shutterstock

Maury Aaseng, 12, 39, 55

© Shelley Gazin/Corbis, 61

© Jim Richardson/Corbis, 6

Shutterstock, 21

D. Silbersweig/Science Source, 26

SPL/Science Source, 53

Thinkstock Images, 17, 28, 33, 45, 48